PRESSURE POINTS

PRESSURE POINTS

How to Survive
Your Stress-Filled World

PETER MEADOWS

WORD PUBLISHING

WORD ENTERTAINMENT LTD
Milton Keynes, England

WORD AUSTRALIA
Nunawading, Victoria, Australia

WORD ENTERTAINMENT LTD
Vancouver, B.C., Canada

STRUIK CHRISTIAN BOOKS (PTY) LTD
Cape Town, South Africa

CAMPUS CRUSADE (ASIA) LTD
Singapore

CHRISTIAN MARKETING NEW ZEALAND LTD
Hastings, New Zealand

JENSCO LTD
Hong Kong

SALVATION BOOK CENTRE
Malaysia

PRESSURE POINTS

Previous editions published 1988 and 1993 by Kingsway
Publications

This revised and updated edition published 1998 by Word
Publishing, 9 Holdom Avenue, Bletchley, Milton Keynes,
Bucks, MK1 1QR, UK.

Reprinted 1998, 2000

ISBN 1–86024–316–9

Produced for Word Publishing by
Bookprint Creative Services, P.O. Box 827, BN21 3YJ, England.
Printed in Great Britain.

Contents

Acknowledgements 7
1 When life goes wobbly 9
2 Stressfully yours 14
3 Blame change and choice 20
4 Life is not always your friend 27
5 High risk? Low risk? 33
6 Action stations 41
7 With attitude 56
8 Sleepless in Suburbia 67
9 Car fumes 72
10 Workers' stress-time 79
11 Growing up with stress 91
12 Church — the time for truth 97
13 Can I have my emotions back, please? 103
14 Truly depressive 116
15 What are we doing to our leaders? 122
16 Rejoice? Are you serious? 135
17 When all else fails, hang on to Dad 141
A discovery evening 146
Notes 151
Bibliography 155

Acknowledgements

My overwhelming thanks are due to the many people without whose contributions this book would have been impossible — either in its original form or this updated and expanded edition.

In particular, take a bow Aredi Pitsiaeli who typed most of the original manuscript, making invaluable observations, and Helen Drain, Fiona Roberts and Jan Todd for inputting the revisions along the way.

My gratitude goes also to all who contributed support, interest, encouragement and advice. They include: Doug and Sue Barnett; Alex and Peggy Buchanan; Clive Calver; Mark and Ruth Dearnley; Steve Gaukroger; Lyndon Bowring; Dr David Hanbridge; Roy Crocker for insights on Moses, Elijah and Jonah; Rob and Di Parsons; Richard Perry; David and Madeleine Potter; Dr Anne Townsend; Dr Lars Morlid; Dr Michael Jones; David and Becky Bellis; and all in the Lifeboat.

Les Stobbe and Barbara Sherrill provided skilful editorial input for the US editon of this book, without which this UK edition would be considerably impoverished.

Peter Meadows
February 1998

1

*My credibility and ability
to survive as a committed Christian
were under threat. I needed
answers to some big questions.*

When life goes wobbly

There is something seriously wrong with our world. Increasing numbers of people are feeling that life is no longer fun.

Just consider these few facts — each with deep personal implications behind the statistics involved.

- More than 90 million working days are lost each year in the UK due to stress-induced illness — costing the British economy £7 billion annually.
- Almost a third of adults feel constantly fatigued — even though many of them have no trouble sleeping.
- A half of all illnesses may have their bases in stress and anxiety.
- One in four — or ten million people — are estimated to be so impeded by stress at work that they are inefficient, accident prone and more likely to take sick leave.

What is going on? Let me illustrate.

Our family was jammed into a huge estate car, eight miles out of Boulogne and heading up the coast road to Calais. Then it happened. For some reason that I could not understand at first, the car which had behaved perfectly during our *gîte* vacation had become unstable and virtually unsteerable.

9

As far as we could tell, the problem had begun earlier in the holiday. A ditch had hurled itself into our path, giving the stabilising bar of the car's suspension a hard knock. There had been no problem at the time — except a red face. But continued pressure and stress finally took its toll. The bar snapped clean through. Now I could give the car all the instructions I wanted via the steering wheel, but it was totally unable to respond.

Life can be like that

We understand how prolonged physical stress can produce that result in something like a car. We also understand how marching soldiers need to 'break step' when crossing a bridge. But we are only just beginning to realise that prolonged and excessive emotional psychological stress can have the same kind of impact on people. Lives may no longer respond to the instructions we give them.

My wife Rosemary and I have shared in that experience. Within months of the birth of our fourth son, surgery revealed that a growth on Rosemary's thyroid was cancerous. Skilful though the surgeon had been, his bedside manner had all the charm of a stealth bomber. That experience, together with the treatment that followed and a string of other negative circumstances — including the death of her father — caused Rosemary's emotions to malfunction.

My vivacious, highly competent, outgoing companion became completely different. She could not bear me to touch her; she'd become almost a recluse; everyday pressures turned into major traumas; she was increasingly irrational and unreasonable. For Rosemary, this meant that, as someone who had previously handled everything thrown at her, she now found even minor pressures overwhelming. These pressures she would have once managed with ease — despite having a growing young family, an over-committed husband, her own small catering company, a hectic social life and a full-scale role within our local church.

We were to discover that there were reasons for this to happen — reasons that this book shares. But we were to discover that few people really understood what we were going through. And, of those who did understand, the majority were unable to be of practical help. Good though our family doctor was, we were left to learn from the storm experience rather than by receiving early warning weather signals as to what might be coming our way.

Big questions

I found myself needing answers to some big questions. Why did others, who seemed to face even greater traumas than ourselves, manage to smile on through? Were Christians like us really expected to remain emotionally unshaken, no matter how hard and often life played a cruel joke? Why were our parents' and grandparents' generations — without all the benefits of modern living — able to cope so much better than we were? And why did people so often look down on someone whose emotions cracked — yet rally in sympathy with those who had physical problems?

This book expresses the answers I have found — and a lot more besides. Intriguingly, it also carries the perspective of my own personal experience.

Having gathered a mass of research on which to begin writing, all I could show for my commitment to the book was an ever-deepening pile of relevant cuttings and notes. With time blanked out in my diary for the great literary assault, our darkness grew darker still.

Up until that point, I had only to cope with the consequences of Rosemary's on-going — though improving —

depressive illness, along with the circumstances that surrounded it. But now my own emotions tripped me up.

For several months I had been waking up exhausted, struggling through the day bowed down by a weariness of body, mind and spirit. All ability to concentrate had gone. My nerves were on edge. I would have given anything for someone to put a volume control on the *Rice Krispies*. Time at my desk often involved little more than rearranging the piles of paper.

As someone who had previously drawn from a bottomless well of boundless energy, it was a shock to be sent home from a major Christian conference, where I was due to lead and speak, to take a complete rest. As one of the conference team assessed eloquently afterwards, 'Your lights were on but there was nobody at home!'

As I began my recuperation and recovery, a consultant psychiatrist told me, 'You are not going to die. It is just that you have been running too close to the edge for far too long.' How right he was.

That painful and personal experience brought a fresh dimension to the research I had gathered. Before, my quest for answers was as a mere spectator. Now I was a participant. If you are 'there' then I have 'been there' too. The following pages are hewn from the hard rock of personal experience.

Gasp for breath

Possibly you have reached out to this book while going through some major set-back. It does not promise to provide instant answers. Indeed, where it does you might not be able to take them in. But in the months to come it should help put your experience into perspective — or prepare you for the next time!

When socked in the stomach, our main concern is to gasp for breath and try to cope with the pain. That is also true when we are 'socked' with life's pressures. We tend to be preoccupied with surviving rather than looking to discover the lessons to be learned from the experience. But there will come a time when you will be ready to view your experience in a different light. And I hope this book proves to be part of that journey.

I would have given anything for a book to help Rosemary and me understand and respond to all we were going through in our times of crisis. If this little volume can meet that need for even one other person, it will have been worth it all.

2 Stressfully yours

God created humankind with all the reflex mechanisms necessary for survival. Our problem is that the world we have created is such that those protective mechanisms are now harming us.

Thank God for stress. Without it you would probably be dead meat by now. Or at least your ancestors would have been. And then there would have been no 'you' at all.

Stress is our survival mechanism. It is the means by which we perform to our peak — particularly in those situations where we see ourselves at risk. The following is a useful definition:

Stress — the changes that take place in your body and mind when a demand seems greater than your ability to cope.

This is all to do with what has become known as the 'fight or flight' instinct. At the first glimpse of danger — of any kind — your brain, without even waiting for permission, begins to equip your body to either 'fight' off the danger or for 'flight' to escape it. Remember those times when your heart has pounded, your face gone white and hands become clammy? These are just outward signs of the 'fight or flight' instinct in action.

At even the slightest whiff that your competence could be at risk, your brain goes to work to protect you by triggering your autonomic (automatic) nervous system. As a result, a wide range of hormones and body chemicals shoot into the bloodstream to give you the added energy, strength and resources you may need.

14

The stars of the show are your adrenal glands. Their big job is creating the adrenalin needed to mobilise the energy reserves of the body. At the same time, your spleen sends out increased numbers of red blood cells providing extra oxygen and nourishment to the muscles and the brain.

Meanwhile the liver is creating vital vitamins, especially B and C, conveying them for fuel to the muscles via the blood. And the stomach is releasing hydrochloric acid, a function normally reserved for digesting food. While physically, your heart begins to pump blood from the outer areas, such as the extremities and skin, and from the stomach to the muscles where it is more needed.

You will notice that your breathing is now faster — in order to generate more oxygen, once again, for the muscles. At the same time, the blood — rather insultingly — is made more able to clot, in preparation for your failure to flee fast enough or to fight with sufficient ferocity. Simultaneously, and almost imperceptibly, the body experiences a tensing of the muscles — again, ready for 'fight' or 'flight'.

Self-survival

What I have described is stress in action. At a threat to your well-being, instinctive reactions prime you for self-survival. Your brain has prepared your body to cope. This is all normal, natural and essential. And very good news. The Bible tells us we are fearfully and wonderfully made (Psalm 139:14). That truth is displayed in the fact that God created humankind with all the reflex mechanisms necessary for survival.

Such a catalogue of actions is a perfectly normal and healthy reaction to an external threat. Indeed, where would we be without it? So why is it that stress in our society is held to be destructive, and branded as the epidemic of the times? Why is stress the reason that life can take a serious wobble for so many?

Our problem is that the world we have created is such that

those protective mechanisms are now harming and even killing us. Stress has become distress.

As we will see over the coming pages, the kind of world that we have created is doing us untold harm. The external danger signals to our brain can be unyielding. The pace of life and its growing demands inflicts a constant charge of adrenalin, blood sugars and fats into our metabolism. Then stress becomes distress — damaging our bodies and our emotions for reasons that you are about to discover. As one person put it, your mind is killing your body.

Power surge

It is rather like starting the car on a cold morning by pulling out the choke to give the extra surge of power needed. But never pushing it in again — leading to waste and poor performance. Or you could think of it in terms of electricity. With the right amount of power you can operate your radio, lights, PC, and all the rest. But too much of exactly the same stuff and the power surge will burn everything out.

All that excessive heart-pumping, blood-thickening, muscle-tensing, body-chemical-flowing accounts for large numbers of physical and emotional illness. Physically, it leads to high blood pressure, heart disease, asthma, indigestion, diabetes, chronic constipation, peptic ulcers and skin rashes.

In the same way, a constant imbalance of body chemicals — which are directly linked to our emotional well-being — is going to lead to feelings we don't want and can't control. Our body chemicals also control our ability to fight off illness when it invades. Malfunction of that system means that we are more likely to be unwell from infections due to our resistance being down and our ability to fight back being impaired.

Emotionally, the impact of stress leads to insomnia, tiredness, headaches, nervous breakdown and depression. Indeed, stress is the major contributor to depressive illness. At this very moment there are some three million people in Great Britain suffering from depression. And each year, eight million medical prescriptions are issued for depressive illness.

About forty years ago the Canadian, Hans Selye, borrowed the word 'stress' from physics to describe the way the body responds to outside events. His work laid the foundation for a new wave of stress researchers like Dr Thomas Holmes and Dr Richard Rahe, of Washington University, who made a study of the way change affects our bodies and our minds. Dr Holmes discovered that people who experienced many dramatic changes in their lives over a short period of time are far more likely to experience illness within the following two years.

The research also demonstrated it is not only adverse events that induce stress. Any outside condition or experience that we must confront, even those that we welcome and enjoy, can cause stress as well.

Intensity of demand

The result of Dr Holmes' and Dr Rahe's findings was the now famous Life Change Units Scale — set out on the next page.

The Scale rates possible events in a person's life according to the amount of stress they induce. The scale lists the death of a marriage partner as the most traumatic experience through which anyone can pass. And even welcome experiences, like the birth of a child or an outstanding personal achievement, will contribute to our level of stress. It does not matter whether the situation is pleasant or unpleasant for it to generate a stress load. What counts is the intensity of personal demand that it creates.

Danger comes when we accumulate too high a score on the scale in too short a time. The greater our total over a six-month period, the more likely it is we will suffer from the symptoms of stress overload. A score between sixty and eighty is considered normal. Over one hundred indicates a lot of

LIFE CHANGE UNITS SCALE[1]

Event	Score
Death of a spouse	100
Divorce	73
Marital separation	65
Prison term	63
Death of a close family member	53
Personal injury or illness	53
Marriage	50
Losing job	47
Marital reconciliation	45
Retirement	45
Change in health of a family member	44
Pregnancy	40
Sex difficulties	39
Gain of new family member	39
Business readjustment	39
Change in financial state	38
Death of a close friend	37
Change to different type of work	36
Change in number of marital arguments	35
Large mortgage or loan	31
Foreclosure of mortgage or loan	30
Change of responsibilities at work	29
Son or daughter leaving home	29
Trouble with in-laws	29
Outstanding personal achievement	28
Spouse begins or stops work	26
Begin or end school or college	26
Change in living conditions	25
Trouble with boss	20
Change in working hours	20
Change in residence	20
Change in school or college	20
Change in recreation	19
Change in church activities	18
Change in social activities	18
Moderate mortgage or loan	17
Change in sleeping habits	16
Change in number of family get-togethers	15
Change in eating habits	15
Holiday	13
Christmas	12
Minor violation of the law	11

stress — high enough to increase a person's susceptibility to illness by up to 80 per cent.

To be more specific, illness can be anticipated in the near future in the following proportions:

over 300 — by almost four out of five;
200 to 299 — by about half;
150 to 199 — by about one in three.

Research revealed that of those with a score between 150 and 300, just over half had suffered recent serious illness. Yet the occurrence of illness rose dramatically to eight out of ten for those with a score over 300. And that was our family's experience.

Into overload

In less than six months, Rosemary had experienced a new baby, the death of her father, a life-threatening medical condition and a number of other 'life changes', including Christmas. She tipped the scale at 315. Her system went into overload and her emotions became unmanageable. The result was the most severe of all the by-products of stress — depression. At the time, it made no sense at all. But now, with the Rahe Scale in front of us, it makes all the sense in the world.

Researchers continue to track this research, which was first released some forty years ago. And while the principle stays constant some small details have changed with time. For example, a similar study in 1997 showed that while top of the hit list used to be 'money, retirement and sex', it is now 'health, relationships and work'. More telling is that those behind this report, published in the *Journal of Psychosomatic Research*, claim that, over the past forty-year period, the overall stress of life appears to have increased by 45 per cent. Who would doubt it?

Indeed, there are significant reasons for our adrenal gland — and all the rest — going into overload, as you are about to see.

3

Gone are families spending their lives within the security and familiarity of a settled group of relatives and friends.

Blame change and choice

Why do past generations appear not to have suffered from stress in the way that this one has? Didn't the condition exist? Or have researchers simply given a name to something that was always there, and found there is money in treating and writing about it?

Of course, stress has always been there. But today there are vital differences. In the past, stress did not exist at its present scale of intensity. At the same time, the lifestyle of our parents and grandparents reduced their vulnerability to its impact.

Today's epidemic was stunningly prophesied in Alvin Toffler's significant best-seller *Future Shock*. Almost thirty years ago, with the Life Change Units Scale to the forefront of his mind, Toffler could see the future. Two major factors, he foretold, would do untold harm: change and choice.

Toffler could see a world where 'change' and 'choice', he predicted, would be in epidemic proportions. And, because our 'fight or flight' mechanism bursts into life each time we encounter them, stress overload was guaranteed. Toffler has been proved right — in spades.

Change

Consider the way we must now cope with the frequency of change. Just glance down the list of stress inducers on the Life

Change Units scale and reflect on how many of them are far more frequent experiences for this generation than for its forebears.

Marriage and divorce. The two go hand-in-hand when it comes to frequency of change. The greater frequency of divorce may not be quite matched by the same number of new marriages, but it is not that far behind. And the new 'living as partners' syndrome sees these committed relationships ending more swiftly and more often than conventional marriage.

Location. We are also a population of people who keep changing location. Two generations ago it was not unusual to find those who had been educated, employed, married, raised a family and buried in the town where they had been born. Today such people are as rare as acne on *Baywatch*.

Indeed, according to a survey by the insurance company Legal & General,[1] two-thirds of the population are likely to live in four or more homes during their adult lives — and half will have already moved away from their roots.

Faced with the need to find a home that is affordable, or employment that is available, multitudes move to environments where everything is new. Gone are families spending their lives within the security and familiarity of a settled group of relatives and friends. People no longer build lifelong friendships with their co-workers.

The world of work. The concept of a job for life has long gone. It is estimated, to keep in the employment market, people will now have to be retrained at least four times in their life. While the present trend is ever more towards short-term contracts, to be secure for more than a few months is all that many can hope for.

Everyday issues

There is also the multitude of change relating to everyday issues that confront us. Each calls into question our ability to function — triggering our 'fight or flight' resources again and again.

Technology. For example, the most stress-filled home is now the one without a five year old to show you how to work the video player. And just when you have got it sorted along comes a new model.

In the stress-inducing world of technology, nothing stays the same for long — particularly now that the office has invaded our homes. In the good old days I had one telephone number. Now there is one for the home, the mobile, the office, and the fax. And don't forget the e-mail address.

Today, we must also cope with the personal computer and its acolytes; photocopiers with a multitude of programmes; fax machines and e-mail that make sending information almost as easy as dialling a phone number. I said 'almost'. And who has not been driven to distraction by the complex multi-functions of memory-store telephones with 'call-waiting', 'divert' and all the rest? We don't use a fraction of the available functions, yet still are driven to distraction.

The technology that is supposed to make our lives easier inflicts a pressure all of its own. And the issue here is not the pressure from trying to cope but the way it all keeps changing. It is not just computer software that upgrades every third Wednesday. Everything seems to be designed with a built in self-destruct mechanism, timed for the moment the warranty is out of date. And the replacement always demands a degree in Science and Technology.

Then there are our encounters with the new wizardry that others impose on us. I have spent hours on end trying to circumvent telephone switchboards that give me only recorded voices and a selection of numbers to press. There are humans in there somewhere if only I can find them.

There is but one glimmer of hope in all this. But only in the world of computers. In the first days of the motor car and electricity, those who used either needed to know almost as much as the manufacturers themselves. Does that sound familiar? What it means is, so far as the computer is concerned, these are still its 'get out and get under' days. The time will come when it all works as smoothly as today's car where you just turn a key and drive. But not yet.

Knowledge. The sum total of what we know keeps changing too. For example, what we discover about our environment affects the products we purchase — from petrol to aerosols to biodegradable packaging. Just when we'd all changed from using aerosols in order to save the ozone layer, they developed one that was environmentally friendly. Knowledge gained from medical research changes our eating habits . . . goodbye cholesterol, hello oat bran. Remember when it was OK to eat beef and to sit out in the sun?

The first four Meadows children came into the world neatly spaced with more or less two years between them. But even in these brief periods, the attitudes and philosophies about infant care constantly changed. One year Rosemary would be encouraged to breast-feed; two years later it was the bottle. Feeding on demand became feeding to a routine. Then, the baby should sleep on its back. On its front. Pick it up. Leave it to yell. Everyone had an opinion based on the current vogue, or whatever magazine article they'd read that week.

Choice

Alongside this world of change is the modern phenomenon of 'overchoice', with its stress-generating effects. It has invaded almost every area of contemporary life — just as Alvin Toffler warned.

In his book *The Want Makers*, Eric Clark notes that in the mid 1970s, the average American supermarket offered the choice of some 9,000 items. By 1985 it was 22,000. Today it is more than 50,000. Clark claims that one month alone saw 235 new items launched on the American market. It seems to me that the UK is not that far behind — if 'behind' is the right word.

In his book *Real Time*, Regis McKenna claims the average American supermarket shopper typically spends twenty-one minutes buying 'an average of eighteen items out of 30,000 to 40,000 choices'. That is because today's computer technology makes it possible to create, test and refine new products at a rate that was previously impossible. As a result, from only a few thousand new products launched each year during the 70s, more than 50,000 came to birth in America. The UK experience is close on their heels.

This is not all the 'fault' of computers. It is also a result of our new global village. As Regis McKenna observes, shelves offer 'such exotic as sake, lemon grass, coconut milk, several brands of black bean and soy sauce, basmati rice, tamarind pods, bok choy, French sea salt, morels, polenta, mangoes, lavosh and Challah bread'.

Indeed, when Jesus taught his followers to pray 'give us this day our daily bread', each one of them would have created the same mental picture of the bread in question. Not so today. The choice at your supermarket includes high fibre, white, hi-bran, wholemeal, country grain, wheat, soft grain, mixed grain, rye, pitta, rolls (bridge, morning, finger, crusty, soft, brown, soft grain, white) and buns. Most likely you can also find fruit breads and a whole range of Italian specialities with unpronounceable names that are not safe to say in mixed company.

Ford Motor Company once made its historic offer, 'You can have any colour so long as it is black.' Those days are long gone. Now the choice options are seemingly limitless. Almost any make available offers at least four engine sizes, five levels of luxury finish, twelve paint colours and three interior styles. Then there are options on wheel trims, stereo systems, the gear box, electric windows and door locks, sun-roof and so on. Multiply the range of choices together and, in effect, the car you finally choose could be one of 25,000 alternatives. That's stress!

Fashion now brings a new set of choices with every season. When our family took a French farm-house vacation, it was after weighing up the competing merits from seventeen different brochures. Two weeks in Florida was the result of days of research — phone, fax, internet — to evaluate the best deal on flights, car hire and accommodation. So different from my childhood week in Kent, picked at random from a dozen options in *Dalton's Weekly*.

When my parents contemplated having a telephone, their decision rested on one issue only — 'Shall we?' There was not even a choice about where the device would go — all telephones went in the hall. As I write, the British Telecom catalogue in front of me offers forty-eight different types of phones, the options encompassing: colour, style, memory facility, clock, automatic re-dial and more. And do I want BT, Cable & Wireless or my local cable company? And who do I choose for my 'friends and family' cheap discount call?

Advertising invasion

All this choice explodes into our homes through the world of advertising. Figures from the Broadcasters Audience Research Bureau reveal that we watch more than 9,000 TV commercials a year. One estimate is that the average person receives around 3,000 advertising messages a day from TV, radio, magazines, posters and the rest. And by the age of eighteen the typical British teenager will have been confronted with some 150,000 television advertisements.

Such advertising issues the challenge to decide. It also promotes a level of success in terms of possession and appearance that people desperately aspire to but will probably never reach. The subconscious is left to work overtime to cope with the unresolvable gap between what we are and what we feel we ought to be — and how the gulf can be bridged.

The problem of 'overchoice' is not limited to our secular

consumer society. Once Bible selection was simply a matter of choosing any copy of the *King James Version* bound in black. Today you will find an almost endless choice of translations, paraphrases, formats and bindings. Any day they will be joined by the 'Exceptionally Good News Bible' and a version printed on waterproof paper for evangelism to deep-sea divers. Then there is the decision as to which Bible software version you want for your PC.

Moral choices. The plethora of choices unique to our generation also includes ethical and moral decisions that are of greater consequence than ever before. Moral dilemmas like test-tube babies, surrogate motherhood, embryo experiments and animal cloning are unavoidable. Issues like this may not demand choices that lead to action, but they do demand choices as to the opinions we hold. These are choices of a complex and overwhelming kind that no other generation has faced. And they get more profound by the hour.

In contrast, Rosemary is convinced that her grandmother went innocently to her grave without ever knowing what a lesbian was. Today we have to face complex choices concerning our attitudes toward 'equal opportunities' and 'positive images' regarding those with homosexual and lesbian lifestyles.

The impact of change and 'overchoice' has crept up so imperceptibly that we have been unaware of what has been happening. It is rather like that well-worn story of the frog and a pan of boiling water. Drop a frog into the bubbling water and it will immediately jump out. But place the frog in while the water is still cold and it will stay there while you gradually warm up the water and boil it to death. We are now at boiling point so far as the way changes and choice impacts our life today.

4

An afternoon cooking in the kitchen has become a few minutes reaching for pre-cooked and packaged dishes.

Life is not always your friend

Three days into a holiday and I'm beginning to get tetchy. The family know the signs and can be found muttering among themselves, 'What's wrong with dad?' In truth, 'tetchy' is probably a very polite word for what has become a grumpy old man with a short fuse. But why should this happen each time I put some significant space in my life? It took me some time to figure out. And then the penny dropped.

The effect of adrenalin pumping through our veins is to create a buzz of confidence and elation. It is an effect that some people crave — almost like an addiction — without realising it. This 'high' is what keeps them going. Cut off the supply by slowing them down and their nerve ends start to jangle. And this was what was happening to me. Like an addict going into withdrawal, my body was screaming 'feed me, feed me', and my nerves were on edge until I was the other side of cold turkey.

This confession has been made to help explain to you why — believe it or not — some people actually create stress for themselves on purpose. In order to feed their adrenalin addiction, they subconsciously defer work until the last minute to create a 'deadline high', create a stressful environment at work, constantly crave fresh challenges, or look for ways to live on the edge during their social hours. And some of that is true of me.

27

In view of all the stress inflicted by change and choice, you may be surprised that anyone needs to create some stress of their own. It is even more surprising when you consider all the other things in life today that are just as stress-inducing.

Indeed, in essence there are four distinct kinds of stress to which we can all be subject. Think of them like this:

● **Stress of the moment**. This comes from an immediate challenge to our ability to cope. It is all about the demand of the moment — from negotiating a difficult road junction to giving a speech, taking a penalty kick to searching for your keys.

● **Stress over time**. This is the ongoing 'nag' from something that you have not been able to resolve. For example, a change in circumstances, the death of someone you love, or a difficult relationship.

It is also to do with the way life is from day-to-day in our frenetic user-unfriendly society. Several of the major issues are about to be faced in detail in this chapter. The others include:

Physical stress from working long hours
Lack of sleep
Hard physical labour
Chronic pain and postural strain
Chemical intake from unwise eating
Medications
Food additives
Artificial sweeteners
Environmental toxins in the air and water

All of these affect the way your body chemicals function and so influence your physical and mental health.

● **Stress caused by concern for the future**. In other words, 'worry'. This is a concern over things that have not yet happened — and might even not. How will the meeting go?

What will be the results of the medical test? Will there be too much month left at the end of the money?

● **Stress from the past**. Most of us have a history that contains things we wish people had not said or done to us, events that we wish had passed us by, and our own regretful failures. This history of old hurts and bad memories can not be rewritten. The only answer is to let it all go.

Any realistic consideration of major stress-inducers needs to include the three that follow.

What we owe. 'If you cannot afford it, don't buy it.' That was the maxim of my own parents and the majority of their contemporaries. In their day, having a bank account was something for the privileged few, and plastic money was a science-fiction fantasy. Almost the only way to get into debt was through the slate at the corner store, the tallyman, or by making a surreptitious visit to the local pawnbroker.

Today, one in ten of all UK households are having trouble repaying debt. For every credit card owned ten years ago, there are three today. During the 1980s the amount owed on bank overdrafts, loans, finance company advances, credit cards and the like more than trebled. And the trend has continued unabated during the nineties.

Today the average family in the UK will be carrying credit card and store card debt of more than £3,000. Debt help lines report the average debt they help people with is nearing £20,000. More than 300,000 people are currently overdue on their mortgage payments by more than three months. While more than three million summonses are issued for personal debt each year.[1]

Such a debt load naturally generates stress. The ordinary person, struggling to survive under their own debt mountain, inevitably pays for the stress involved. Here is something for which the 'fight or flight' instinct is usually nigh on impossible. It is a price that few in previous generations ever encountered.

Increased expectations. A significant by-product of the wide range of technological advances is the new expectations that they place on us. Take the washing machine for instance. Has it really made life so much easier?

There was a time when it was common and socially acceptable to wear the same clothes several days in a row, or for several days in the same month. But the time eventually came when there was a washing machine in almost every home. The higher standards of cleanliness it now offers means not to wear a freshly washed shirt to work is almost unthinkable.

In a similar way, the progress made by the personal computer has made life both easier and harder at the same time. Today, no one gives a second thought to making the umpteenth revision to a completed document — because it is technically so easy. But the result is that no document, report or letter is ever really counted as finished.

At the same time, take a moment — that is all you are allowed these days — to muse on some of the areas of life that make life 'instant' and so establish expectations as to the way life should be. There's everything from fax invasion to twenty-four hour telephone banking.

These higher standards of service have now established expectations as to the way it has to be for everyone else. Once schedules assumed that everything would take two days to pass from place to place. Today, the availability of instant fax and e-mail, and before 9am next day delivery means this is now the way almost everything is expected to be done. We just have to figure out a way to live with the pressure involved.

The pace of life. We have also been called the 'now' generation. No matter what it is, we want it now and we must do it now. Instant coffee, noodles, bank information, and all the rest have robbed us of those natural 'oases' which used to permeate the existence of previous generations.

A half-hour bus ride to the shops has become a five-minute car ride with its attendant frustrations. An afternoon cooking in the kitchen has become a few minutes reaching for pre-cooked and packaged dishes — with the time saved being used to make the choices and to absorb the stress-inducing information needed to survive today.

The significance of all this is not only are we being bombarded with ceaseless stimuli, we have lost the time needed to let our body chemicals settle down to normal again.

The truth of this hit me at a time when I was desperately trying to get some rest and relaxation to deliver me from burn-out. I parked my car in nearby Richmond Park, resolving to do nothing at all other than walk in the April sunshine.

After two and a half hours (that seemed more like two and a half weeks) of forcing myself to walk slowly, breathe deeply and stop twitching, it was time

Life is out to get you

Here are some of the things that now define the speed at which we are expected to function:

- instant money from hole in the wall
- round-the-clock telephone banking
- pizza delivery
- the fax
- the microwave
- twenty-four hour TV news
- drive-through fast food restaurants
- one hour spectacle and contact lens manufacture
- next day office supply delivery
- reach-me-any-time-and-anywhere mobile phones

for lunch. As unhurriedly as many years of bad habit would allow, I joined the queue in the park's self-service cafeteria, thankful that it was making progress at the same funereal rate I had set for myself.

Eventually I came face to face with the young assistant who had been keeping us all entertained with his brisk and effective response to all requests.

'I'll have the special baked potato, please.' The words came out as slowly as I could manage.

The assistant took my order and placed my soon-to-be-lunch in a small oven with a timer. He then announced, with abject apology, what he obviously expected to be devastating news: 'I am afraid it will take forty-five seconds.'

5

Physically some of us bruise more readily than others, and the same is true of our emotional make up.

High risk? Low risk?

I've got good news and bad news. The good news is that we are not all equally at risk from the effects of prolonged stress. The bad news is that some of us are considerably more vulnerable than others. Two seemingly identical people may face an equal barrage of circumstances, with each taking the same evasive action, and one may come through unscathed while the other crumbles.

How can that be? The answer is that our vulnerability factor relates to our personality type, our gender, our genes and our life-role. By understanding our own place on the stress-risk scale, we discover how seriously the threat must be regarded and what action to take.

Your personality

There are those whose very personality makes them vulnerable and at risk. The American cardiologists Friedman and Roseman divided people into Type A and Type B personalities. They discovered that a Type A is between two and five times more likely to have a heart attack.

Type A's are strong-willed, goal-orientated people, self-confident, driven by ambition, and hating routine. More than that, they are enthusiastic and thrive on challenge. All this sounds wonderfully attractive until viewed with the rest of the picture.

The bad side is that Type A's are demanding of themselves and others, often very materialistic, and always seem pressured and rushed. They have a tendency to be critical, aggressive, hostile and more interested in work than family. Type A people also tend to hide their feelings, tackle more than one task at a time, interrupt before people finish their sentences, eat quickly, focus on their own wants and generally overlook the positive achievements of those who work for them. None of this is very nice.

Tragically, our society holds up Type A people as role models of commitment and success — people we should all strive to emulate. All-working, no-playing, hard-driving, winning-at-all-costs people are the heroes of our public life and business institutions. Many of us have been fooled into believing that this is the way we ought to behave to be authentic achievers.

Are you a Type A?

Type A personality people are:
    strong-willed
    goal-oriented
    perfectionist

They:
    hate routine
    thrive on challenge
    do more than one thing at a
        time

And are:
    at least twice as likely to suffer a
        heart attack

But not all Type A's are driven by materialistic gain. Many are equally motivated by idealism. At least, this is my own excuse for my own moderate Type A personality. Money and possessions have never beckoned. But give me a cause to fight for and watch the dust fly.

Type A people may simply be desperate to feel needed and affirmed by others. Often they believe their value comes only from what they achieve, or they are only worth what they own.

Action points for Type A's

- Schedule time for your family and yourself — and keep the appointment.
- Don't take work with you on a break or a holiday.
- Schedule regular creative lunch-breaks. Visit places you would like to see or just find a place to sit and relax.
- If you are working, use time away from the office as private time.
- Go into work early or stay late rather than taking work home.

Perhaps the most unfortunate thing of all is that Type A's treat their cars with more respect and thoughtfulness than they do their own bodies. And pay the price.

Can Type A people change their personality? Probably not completely, and certainly not significantly after the age of twenty-five. But they can recognise the risk involved and act accordingly. Owning up to the kind of people that they are is the first step. Making a conscious effort to put life into a more realistic perspective is the second.

The Lord Jesus Christ had a lot to say about the Type A personality. He told the parable of the man driven by business success — tearing down small barns and building bigger ones. But the moment he was at the very height of self-satisfaction, his creator blew the whistle to call 'time'. Jesus also made the statement which runs contrary to everything the world would have us believe. He said, 'A man's life does not consist in the abundance of his possessions' (Luke 12:15, NIV).

Male or female?

In a competitive working environment, men appear to experience the effects of stress more than their female counterparts. A key is possibly the way men resist expressing their emotions in a world where 'big boys don't cry'.

Stress counsellor Richard Young, recommends that companies wanting senior executive staff had better look more seriously at women. In his judgement, 'It is possible that they deal with stress better because they are more ready to talk it over.'[1]

In contrast, it is on the home front that a woman is usually the most vulnerable. Here *she* is expected to be competent. A Finnish study, for example, reveals that when a couple takes their child to casualty, it is the wife whose adrenalin level soars the highest. She is the one who regards this as an area in which she should be able to cope.

Britain's social psychiatrist, Dr Paul Bevington, points out that it is the woman who takes responsibility for the emotional side of the family — organising birthdays, reminding her husband to keep in touch with his family, planning Christmas and family traditions[2]. She also faces the stress of seeing her husband get an unfair share of the credit.

Studies show that women suffer from anxiety and depression two and a half times more frequently than men. And it is those women at home with young children who inflate this statistic — with single-parent mothers being the leading contenders. To be specific, married women, particularly those with young children, are four times as likely to experience depression as is a single woman.

The working mother may experience the release from stress that comes from getting out of the house. But this is too often replaced by the guilt of abandoning her children to others as well as the exhaustion of returning home to start another full day's work.

Your make-up

Some people are far less resilient than others to the strains and stresses of life — be it in their joints or their emotional make up. Physically some of us bruise more readily than others, and the same is true of our emotional make up.

The way our adrenal gland stands up under pressure is a major factor in how we will fare. And people inherit their glandular patterns in the same way that they acquire their hair colour or the shape of their nose. This means that the less fortunate inherit weaker adrenal glands which are more likely to stress out under pressure.

The lesson here is to avoid the temptation to look down on those who crumble under a load that is lighter than the one being carried by those who are coping. Or to be intimidated by those who seem to be able to bear a weight greater than yours. It is all down to the way that their genes are scrambled.

Where the control is

Those who face the greatest stress are those without the right or ability to control what is happening to them. A perfect illustration of this appeared in a *Newsweek*[3] cover story on stress. This quoted a study of racing-car drivers conducted by Rick Gilkey, an associate professor of organisational behaviour at Emory University's School of Business Administration in America.

Gilkey discovered that the moment when drivers were under the greatest stress was not when they were speeding at 200 miles an hour, nor when battling for the lead or when heading for the flag. It was during the pit-stops, when the work crew controlled things. In other words, when their destiny was in the hands of others stress levels were the highest.

An American survey published in the *British Journal of Medical Psychology*[4] takes this concept further, showing that the people who are really stressed in the workplace are more likely to be telephone operators, waiters, fire-fighters, cashiers and cooks — because they have little power to make decisions while the psychological demands on them are high.

What we learn is that someone on a production line faces more stress than the executive manager to whom they report, because the manager has at least some power to control his workload. High demands but with no control as for the waiter, check-out assistant, traffic officer, taxi driver, mother with pre-school children — means tension and stress. High demands with control as for the orchestra conductor, executive, fore-man, truck driver — promises a more reasonable existence.

The church

While no one is immune from stress, those whose lives include being part of the family of the church are additionally at risk.

What should be shelter from the storm can all too easily create a storm of its own. The church causes stress from:

- the guilt that results from falling under the influence of stress;
- the workload for those actively involved in the life of their church;
- the effect of divided loyalties.

Let's look at these in turn.

Guilt. This is all to do with the underlying belief that Christians are supposed to cope with absolutely everything no matter what. And that prayer and faith should always be enough to see us through. This is such a damaging concept that it deserves looking at in depth — which is what I do in chapter 13.

Workload. The largest cause of stress in Christian homes, according to a survey, is church responsibility.

The blame for this high level of stress cannot all be laid at the door of over-zealous or unthinking local church leaders who dump on people. There is also a plethora of husbands and wives who 'escape' from family responsibilities under the dis-guise of spiritual activity. No amount of sympathy is enough for the wife who finds herself screaming at her man, 'Adam's sick, the grass is six inches deep, the washing machine has spewed water all over the kitchen floor and you tell me you are going to the *!#! deacons' meeting!'

Particularly vulnerable to over-commitment are couples who have grown up through the church and now find themselves with a young family. Once they were free to spend many hours in church activity. Now they are expected — and feel compelled — to maintain the same work-rate without any consideration for their new responsibilities as parents. Moreover, everyone else around them seems to be coping with their workload — surely they can as well.

Divided loyalties. The Christian couple is often torn between the demands of two masters — their commitment within the church and their responsibility to their family. The homemaker-wife who sees her zealous husband bolt his meal and dash off to save the world feels guilty over the resentment she feels for being abandoned. She loves God, wants to serve him, and wants her husband to serve him too. But she wants 'him' — and feels so incredibly guilty for resenting the times when she is left literally holding the baby while he is out being busy for God. She longs for his time, touch and undivided attention.

At the same time, this husband is on the rack — stretched between his commitment to his family and his promises to 'the deacons'. 'They' will never understand if he doesn't deliver to their level of expectation. So 'she' will have to understand — and make the adjustments when he is not there.

Not that the workload in churches should fall only on the shoulders of singles, couples without children and those whose offspring have left the nest. It is these categories — particularly the singles — who already are too quickly dumped on with every new responsibility and project that emerges.

There is a world of difference between self-sacrifice through genuine discipleship and the actions of those who constantly take their partners, or their parents, for granted. Forsaking everything for the sake of Jesus and the gospel must go hand in hand with Paul's command that husbands should love their wives to the same measure that Jesus loves the church (Ephesians 5:25).

Robbery

John Mallison is a Bible teacher and small-group expert. He tells the story of being at a retreat for ministers in his native Australia. Those present were divided into groups in order to share in a relational Bible study on the parable of the Good Samaritan. The idea was that each person would try to identify with a character in the parable, explaining what they learned from trying to get inside that person's skin.

One by one the group went through the various characters — the priest, the Levite, the Samaritan, the innkeeper. They may even have done the donkey for all I know. The session was all but finished and about to break up when John pulled them back together. 'There is one person we failed to look at,' he protested. 'What about the robbers?'

God had been convicting John at the very deepest level. Those robbers were just like him. He had robbed his wife and his family of himself and his time — with the service of God used as justification.

John went back to his conference centre room and wrote separate letters of apology and repentance to his wife and family. His wife told him afterwards, 'Only the Holy Spirit could have revealed that to you.'

We need that kind of revelation in our families and our churches if we are to free countless Christian wives and husbands from a burden of stress and guilt that should not be theirs.

So now we have seen the cause for today's stress epidemic and identified those most at risk. But what can be done?

6

You do not have to lie down and allow the ravaging impact of stress to jump all over you. You can fight back.

Action stations

We have seen what life at the end of the twentieth century is like. But the big issue is: 'What are we going to do about it?'. Interestingly, all around us are people who recognise the problem and are beginning to respond. Indeed, the top selling book of 1997 was *The Little Book of Calm* by Paul Wilson.

This little pocket-sized book, with a piece of anti-stress advice on every page, sold more than 450,000 copies. Can we do better than the advice it dispenses which includes — 'Pretend it's Saturday', 'Sell your wrist-watch' and 'Wear Donald Duck underpants'? I think we can.

I claim no professional qualifications that give me the right to hand out advice on how to deal with stress. But as a sufferer — as well as a carrier (!) — I am well able to recognise good advice on the subject. As a result, the following pages draw from the work of no less than twenty professional doctors and counsellors, as well as countless publications and articles. Also thrown in are a bunch of ideas that are working for me.

First, you need to judge how critical is your need to take action. One national magazine ran its own light-hearted list of tell-tale signs of being overstretched. This included: 'you sleep like a baby — you wake up every two hours crying'; 'you start biting other peoples' fingernails'; and 'leisure time is stopping at traffic lights.'

You have probably already checked yourself against the Life Change Units Scale. This tells you how much you are at risk. Another indicator is the following list of symptoms indicating stress.

YOUR 'STRESS-SIGN' CHECK LIST

	Often	Too Often
Physical		
indigestion or heartburn		
breathlessness without exertion		
waking up tired		
sweaty hands		
excessive perspiration		
racing heartbeat		
chronic constipation or diarrhoea		
persistent headaches		
muscular twitching or cramps		
frequent blushing		
dry mouth and problems with swallowing		
Emotional and mental		
boredom		
feelings of futility or low self-worth		
'blue' moods		
feeling isolated and misunderstood		
lack of interest in life		
unreasonable fears		
fear of open or closed spaces		
fear of being alone		
lack of ability to unwind		
sudden attacks of panic		
disturbing dreams		
forgetfulness or confusion		
Behavioural		
insomnia		
tendency to avoid people		
erratic eating habits		
disinterest in sex		
irritability		
loss of sense of humour		
outbreaks of irrational anger		
difficulty in making decisions		
misuse of alcohol		
deep sighing		
lack of concentration		
irresponsible behaviour		
grinding your teeth		
lack of interest in appearance/hygiene		
fidgeting		
an increased number of minor accidents		

If you find yourself ticking several items in this list, feel positive rather than negative. At least you have identified warning signals. Now you have the opportunity to take action before it's too late.

No matter where you find yourself on the stress-risk scale, you do not have to lie down and take it. Yes, you may face an epidemic bombardment. True, the intensity of unresolved pressures, threats and choices is without precedence. But, you can fight back.

Of course you do not have to take the positive action needed. Instead, you could mask the symptoms — using pills for your heart pains, antacid tablets to fight indigestion, ointments to ease skin rashes, props like nicotine and alcohol and so on. However, while you will feel better in the short-term, the problem has not gone away. In fact, what you will have done is about as wise as unscrewing the shining red oil warning light from your car's dashboard because of its irritating effect. Just like an engine without oil, you will be heading for the certain danger of grinding to a nasty halt.

So let's be more positive. The following chapter focuses on the attitudes you need. But first we will look at the actions required to limit the stress that comes your way — and to reduce its impact when it does.

Your lifestyle

Eat a well-balanced diet. Eat at least one well-balanced meal each day. Starchy foods like pasta, rice, potatoes and bread are good for energy. You also need a good supply of vitamins — from foods like holoenzyme cereals, vegetables and fish.

Eat slowly, chew thoroughly and don't gulp your food. Reduce or even stop all drug stimulants like coffee, tea, alcohol and tobacco.

Exercise regularly. A short, brisk walk twice a week is enough to make a noticeable difference. Sensible exercise puts to use the physical changes that stress inflicts. A good work-out will literally help you get stress out of your system. Stimulating the body through exercise also causes the brain to manufacture endorphins — natural opiate-like substances that can lift your mood and give feelings of well-being.

Psychiatrist Dr Desmond Kelly, President of the International Stress Control Society, says, 'There is no doubt that for many people aerobics burns up the adrenalin which is produced by too much stress and also helps counteract the damaging effects of anger, which is often a part of depression. I sometimes suggest an exercise bike if [my clients] are feeling angry — within five or ten minutes the anger subsides and they feel a lot better.'[1]

Establish sensible sleep habits. Sleep a regular eight hours each night. Remember that longer can be counter-productive, and an hour before midnight is worth two after.

Slow down. Try putting a small coloured spot on your watch, steering wheel or telephone handset. When it catches your eye, take a moment to check your tension, relax your shoulders and ease your pace.

Do something enjoyable. Make sure you have a hobby or spend regular time doing something you enjoy for the sheer fun of it. Going to the theatre, reading, model-making, watching sports, painting, cooking, gardening are all good examples. Even sitting quietly with your feet up qualifies.

But don't rely on a succession of quiet evenings in front of the TV as being a barrier to stress. Research suggests that the longer people watch the box the more drowsy, bored and hostile they become. The thirteen-year study by two research psychologists at Chicago university found that people who used their TV sets to relax were less relaxed by the time they eventually turned them off.[2]

For those who have decided to live as a follower of Jesus, such a step does not mean abandoning normal social and recreational life. A past generation would often quote 'The devil finds work for idle hands to do' — and back it up by pointing out that Jesus and his disciples never stopped for breath or the Palestinian equivalent of a game of squash.

In fact, the lifestyle of Jesus presents a splendid example to our stress-filled world. As Gordon MacDonald points out: 'When he went from town to town with his disciples, he moved on foot (or in a boat). There were long hours of quietness in the countryside those walks. It wasn't frantic jetting around — breakfast in Jerusalem, lunch in Damascus and supper in Antioch.'[3]

You will also find Jesus taking time for long relaxed meals, weddings, breakfast with his friends. And, true to the example of Jesus, the apostle Paul had no sense of guilt over taking time to wait in a city to be joined by his companions (Acts 17:16).

MacDonald underlines the fact that 'the pace of life in Jesus' time was automatically governed not by inner discipline but by practical obstacles that we have overcome by high-speed transportation, telephone and organisational technique'.

Don't go it alone. This stress-filled world is not a place to try to survive on our own. We need each other. However, for whatever reason, most people end up putting their life roots down into soil that is geographically far away from where they grew up. The result is to be isolated from the relatives and the friends with whom they grew up, and robbed of the help needed in order to cope with the effects of stress when they come.

Previous generations were born and buried in the same community. Sisters, brothers, aunts, uncles, grandparents and close friends all lived close enough to make valuable contributions to the welfare of the family. Baby-sitting circles did not exist in the days of pre-suburban mobility. They were just not needed.

Rosemary and I are among the millions who grew up in

homes where a granny, aunt or uncle lived with us. That extended family provided the necessary relief during times of illness, pressure and stress. Greater mobility is one of the factors that has changed all that. One of the key ingredients for stability and well-being has been eroded in our modern society. And we need strategies to cope. It is simply unrealistic to crash on pretending that we are equipped to go it alone.

The way our world is, we need to build communities of relationships that compensate for the fact that our kith and kin are seldom on hand to share the load and take the pressure. Establish a small network of trusted people who can ease your pressure and be a sounding board to give you confidence in your own judgement. We are not inadequate for failing to cope by ourselves. We were simply not designed to carry on that way.

Make space. When life runs too fast it can demand a drastic response. I can vividly recall a personal pressure point one spring Sunday morning. The previous months had seen me run ragged through trying desperately to cope with the conflicting responsibilities of job and family while Rosemary was extremely unwell. And I was completely done in.

On that particular Sunday morning I had left Rosemary resting at home and had dropped off the children at the children's department of the lovely Anglican church we were attending. There was just one problem. I began to realise that, far from being able to join the congregation for worship, I desperately needed an oasis greater than a Sunday service would provide.

The wave of guilt that swamped me was enormous. But such was my drive for survival that it took only moments to turn the negative into a positive. There was at least an hour before I needed to collect the children — and that hour could be all mine.

Having swiftly purchased my favourite Sunday papers, I sped to the local Happy Eater and ordered the biggest breakfast on the menu. Never have unhurried minutes been so welcome, nor a 'Thank you, Lord' more genuine and meaningful.

Take your medicine. If things get out of control, or show no signs of improving, seek professional advice. Your GP is the place to start. If you are not met with sympathy and understanding, ask to be referred to a specialist. Just the step of telling someone how you feel can do a lot to ease the pressure.

If your doctor prescribes anti-depressant drugs as part of your treatment, don't feel guilty. These medications are not tranquillisers to subdue a patient, but they are a way of getting the brain chemicals to work properly again so that stress management, relaxation and professional counselling can play their part in recovery.

Whatever medical advice you are given, follow it to the letter. One of the great barriers to recovery from the impact of stress is the temptation to give up on treatment the moment you begin to feel better. See it through to the end.

Your stress reducers

So far as practical action to reduce your level of stress, try these for starters.

- Spread out or hold off the major changes and challenges that you face. Does it all have to happen right now?
- Reduce your mortgage or find other ways to lessen your financial commitments. For a definite time, choose to put your resources into 'needs' rather than 'wants'.
- Avoid creating a log-jam of things that need your decision.
- Aim to define your worries and turn them into concrete problems. Worries nag away, but problems can be tackled.
- Don't leave decisions hanging over you. If something has to be done, do it now.

- Stop trying to do more than one thing at a time. Take jobs in order and plan ahead.
- Review your priorities. As Jesus said, what good would it be if you gained the whole world — or that particular part you have your eye on — and lose what is really valuable?
- Don't accept or set yourself impossible deadlines. Does it really have to be done by then?
- Adopt a 'granny' figure who could share in the workload of the home.
- Surround yourself with restful colours.
- Have a massage. A good pummelling promotes blood circulation, relaxes muscle tension and drives out stress from the system.
- Get a pet. Those with pets — particularly dogs — are less likely to suffer from stress-induced illness. But avoid a dog with fleas.

Home help. In our own home, the biggest breakthrough came when we made the decision to hire domestic help in the form of a local sixth form student from 4.30–6.30pm every weekday. In one stroke this settled my constant and often unresolvable dilemma as to whether I should be at home helping out or at the office getting my work done. And it rescued Rosemary from both pressure and guilt.

Of course, there is a certain stress in finding the right help. The 'sharp' way is to phone a local secondary school, asking them to recommend someone bright who would like the experience for a couple of weeks. If it works out then keep them. If not, there is no problem in saying goodbye.

Learn to say 'no'. Our own busyness may have a lot to do with simply failing to say 'no'. This might be because:

We wrongly believe that our value is seen in what we do. Much of our work load can stem from an insatiable need to fill gaps in our lives because we feel incomplete, unloved and unvalued. A greater confidence in the fact that we are cherished and

The seven steps to saying 'no'

1. Make up your mind before any request is likely to come. It is easier to set boundaries when not confronted with specific requests.

2. If caught unaware, at least play for time by, asking for more information or a chance to think it over.

3. Remind yourself that if they feel they have the permission to ask, you have the permission to say no. You are free to set your own priorities, express your own opinions, assert your own values — without feeling guilty or selfish.

4. Deliberately speak slowly, steadily and warmly to avoid the danger of sounding rude and abrupt.

5. Say 'no' clearly, firmly and without any long-winded explanation, invented excuses or self-justification. It might help to own up to your feelings — 'I feel embarrassed about this, but I'm going to have to say "no"' or 'I feel guilty saying "no", but that's the answer I'm going to have to give.'

6. Stick to your statement, repeating it as often as is necessary to get your message across.

7. Don't hang around. To do so could send out misleading signals and encourage those who are asking to try to persuade you to change your mind.

appreciated by God and others would deliver us from the pressing need to 'do' in order to gain approval.

The value of any object has nothing to do with the price tag it carries. The real issue is, what will someone pay? The price God paid for your life was his Son. No matter how worthless we may feel, the fact of what God did through Jesus establishes our real worth.

We have also been created with individual talents, gifts, characteristics and temperaments. We are the pinnacle of the creation that God declared as 'very good'. To fill our lives with activity so as to win the approval and recognition from others is both belittling to our creator and totally unnecessary.

We fail to recognise that saying 'yes' to 'this' means saying 'no' to 'that'. Time does not expand to accommodate each new commitment we make. Each day remains twenty-four hours long, no matter how many extra promises tumble from our well-meaning lips. Time is one of the most precious resources at our disposal. Spend it wisely and remember — you can only spend each minute once.

We wrongly believe that if we don't say 'yes', the job will not get done. Jesus would have been no stranger to that kind of pressure. As he made his way steadfastly to Jerusalem, it takes little imagination to reconstruct the possible words of his disciples walking the same road.

'Master, there is a village close by where many need to be healed.'

'There is a distraught family, Master, where you could bring such a change. It won't take long.'

'Think of the difference you can make! It's not far out of our way.'

Yet Jesus kept going to Jerusalem. Luke tells us that 'Jesus resolutely set out for Jerusalem' (Luke 9:51, NIV). Jesus was able to say no because he had already said 'yes'. Because he knew where he was going, Jesus could be free from having to take on everything else. Jesus knew what we need to know–a need does not always equal a call. The question is, 'What is our own Jerusalem?'

We wrongly believe saying 'no' is selfish, small-minded and even rude, and to do so will leave the person who asked feeling hurt and rejected. We fail to realise that to say no is only to refuse a request, not to reject a person.

Take time for yourself. A significant landmark in my own battle over stress was when I began to schedule time in my appointment book for 'me'. Before my experience with stress overload I had felt too guilty to take that kind of time off. Now I know I will eventually inflict more pressure on those around me if I don't.

What Rosemary does not know until she reads this is that very occasionally — and I mean 'very' — I catch a morning train half-an-hour earlier than I need to. This makes time for my treat. A cooked breakfast in a greasy spoon cafe. But without the fried bread of course.

Learn to Laugh. The feeling of well being and 'lightness' that follows a good work out can be replicated through a good bout of prolonged belly laughter. That is because laughter not only changes how we feel, research over the past ten years has found that laughter causes healthy physical changes to the body.[4]

When we laugh, our tear glands produce moisture, the heart beats faster, the muscles contract, breathing deepens, muscle tension soon eases and our heart then assumes a more relaxed pace. Laughter also creates a decrease in levels of stress

---

Time for you?

To check how much time you are really giving to yourself, make a list of the everyday things you really enjoy.

Be specific — soft-boiled eggs, walking in the park, Simply Red records, eating at a special restaurant, being alone.

When you have ten or so items, tick off those you have experienced over the past month.

The fewer the ticks, the more reason to ask whether you are getting enough time for yourself.

hormones while releasing the body's natural pain killers, endorphins. In short, laughter makes a positive contribution to our biochemical, hormonal and circulatory functions.

No wonder someone has described laughter as 'jogging of the internal organs'. Indeed, one medical doctor who has made a study of the physical benefits of laughter discovered that 100 laughs is equivalent to 10 minutes rowing or jogging.

So important is laughter in the healing process that there is even an American Association for Therapeutic Humour, complete with its own journal. While self-proclaimed 'mirthologist'. Steven M Sultanoff, PhD, is a licensed psychologist and therapeutic 'humor-ist'.

Dr Sultanoff presents his distinct perspective on therapeutic humour at conferences filled with cartoons, jokes, anecdotes, props, stories, quotes, and experiences. The aim is to show how humour reduces stress, provides perspective, improves communication, energizes, enhances relationships, and changes our feelings, thinking, behaviour, and our biochemistry to help us lead healthier and happier lives.

Your ways to relax

However hard you work at it, some stress overload in going to seep under your defences. The best way to fight it off is to learn ways to relax in depth.

If you don't think it is important, just remember in a study of just over 100 heart patients, of those who had learnt relaxation techniques, less than one in ten had a further heart attack in the next five yours. Those who only took more exercise were twice as likely to have a second attack. And those who did nothing were three times as likely.

So listen up! Here are some ways you can learn to relax.

Take time to be quiet each day. Shut out the world for fifteen minutes or so each day. Sit quietly, relax and pray.

Breathe more slowly. Breathing deeply and slowly is one of the quickest and easiest ways to reverse the effects of stress. It is something you can do at any odd moment–and it does make a remarkable difference.

Breathing that is too shallow can induce stress into your system. Breathe from your stomach and not your chest. Count slowly to four or five as you breathe in, then breathe out again in the same way. Use this technique to respond to any stressful situation.

Practise deep relaxation. The aim is to give your mind a rest from thinking about the problems that have caused stress. This, in turn, gives your body time to de-tox from the overload of body chemicals that has built up.

All you need is a quiet, warm room with no bright lights. Sit or lie comfortably, breathing, slowly, regularly and deeply and choose an approach that works best for you. For example:

- *Focusing on an object*: Look at a selected object in immense detail for an extended time. Look at its shape, colour, texture, movement and so on. Try using a flower, a candle, a desk lamp or a tree.

- *Breathing*: Focus your attention on your breathing by counting your breaths from 0 to 9. Picture the numbers changing with each breath.

- *Imagery*: Create a mental picture of a lovely place, using all your senses. See it, hear it, smell it, feel it. Let it sweep over you. Or look at an object and then try to recreate it in your mind's eye with your eyes closed.

At first you will find it hard to keep focused, with your brain darting here and there. Don't worry. Just stick at it.

Relax your muscles. Simply tense up a group of muscles — try it with your hand — as tightly as possible for a few seconds. Then consciously relax them as much as you can. You can use this simple idea on every area of your body to relax and unwind. For maximum effect use this exercise in conjunction with other methods of relaxation.

Be continually filled with the Holy Spirit. Essentially, to be filled with the Holy Spirit means being sure to keep a clear conscience before God — submitting to his rule in every area of your life, and asking him to fill you with his peace, power and presence.

It is from this inner resource of strength that our ultimate ability to survive will come. Yet, being filled with the Holy Spirit will not shield you from limping when you twist your ankle. Likewise, it will not prevent you from the impact of emotional pain.

The question has been posed, 'Can someone filled with the Spirit ever wake up in a bad mood?' It is best answered with another question: 'Can anyone filled with the Spirit ever wake up with a stiff neck?'

Yet the presence of God filling our life is guarantied to make a difference, bringing a level of calm and self-control that would otherwise be outside our grasp. Of course there will be times when our emotional turmoil is such that it seems to wipe out the effectiveness of God's spirit in our lives. There will also be those moments when, without even realising it, we cope at a level that would otherwise have been beyond us — due to what God, by his Spirit, is doing within us.

'Dad, there is water pouring through the ceiling. Come quick!' That brief, telephoned plea spelled the end of our small group Bible study for the evening. Within minutes, Rosemary and I were back at home, with the rest of the group close behind.

Every towel, tray and bowl had been called into play as our four sons fought to keep the effect of the flood to a minimum. Walls were soaked through. The electricity had fused. Everything was chaos.

To our relief, the water was no longer streaming from beneath the new bath installed earlier in the day. But my phone call to the plumber was met with the insistence that he was going out for the evening and 'tomorrow morning will have to do'.

It was an argument that the plumber lost. The mopping up was still under way when he arrived, without apology, to repair his faulty workmanship.

Finally a semblance of peace settled over our dishevelled home. I sat numbly in our kitchen as one of our helping friends reflected how astounded the plumber must have been to meet, in my friend's words, my calm, reasoned and unvindictive manner. In his judgement, almost everyone else would have fed the plumber, limb by limb, into the food processor. 'You had every reason to be steamingly angry,' he said. 'Instead the plumber met Jesus.'

In truth, it must be told that I am, by temperament, a frustratingly placid individual. But I began to recognise that night that God's Spirit in me had made a response possible, in a very pressured situation, that was beyond my own natural and reasonable ability. No credit is due to me. The difference came from the contribution God has made to my life. That dimension can be yours too as you let God fill you with his Holy Spirit.

Now, having looked at some of the things we can do to respond to the reality of stress, what about the attitude we need?

7

A parent who never expressed appreciation, said, 'Well done' or 'I'm proud of you' can leave an indelible mark.

With attitude

There is much more to facing stress in life than the right diet and exercise routine. Indeed, it could be that the attitudes on which your life is founded are the most vital part of the picture — as I hope you are about to see.

Take charge of your life

Keeping stress at bay involves treating yourself as someone with a right to a life of your own. That will involve a degree of assertiveness and confrontation. Those very words can conjure up images of a shoot-out at the OK Corral. It does not have to be that way. There is a world of difference between being assertive and being aggressive.

Sadly, many who need to break out from being always submissive to the expectations and demands of others can only imagine that the alternative is to be aggressive. While the real alternative is to be assertive — something entirely different.

You are submissive when:
- you are not willing or not able to express your feelings, needs, values and personal concerns;

- you let others invade your personal space and trample your rights.

You are aggressive when:
- you tend to stomp over other people;
- you inflict and impose your views and values on others, expressing your feelings at their expense.

You are assertive when:
- you say what you want, without overwhelming or abusing other people;
- you are clear about your own position and let other people know;
- you can accept that others may have views different to yours and may wish to negotiate their position accordingly.

Assertiveness involves much more than defending your rights. It equally concerns being prepared to expect that your own needs be recognised and met. In particular, two key statements typify the maturity of character that lies behind being assertive. These are the convictions that:

I have the right to decide for myself whether or not I am responsible for finding a solution to someone else's problem — and they have the same right when faced with mine.

I have the right to deal with people without having to make them like me — and they have the same right concerning me.

Few people find that assertiveness comes easy. But the hard work involved in self-monitoring your personal style — together with some training through a local evening class or appropriate reading — pays dividends. This is because mastering assertiveness leads to:

- better and more honest communication;
- giving others greater dignity and respect;

- learning to relax and reduce anxiety;
- getting more of your needs accepted;
- closer interpersonal relationships;
- taking responsibility for what happens in your life;
- feeling better about yourself;
- protection from being taken advantage of by others.

There is one other and vital dimension to the issue of assertiveness. There are people who imagine any expression of their own rights and feelings will be seen as nothing more than unrighteous anger. They are constantly over-sensitive to what other people think — especially about them; are constantly anxious to please and so find it hard to express their own views or to disagree with others. Professor Richard Winter points out, 'There are some people who have a particular problem in asserting themselves and coping with anger and they are especially vulnerable to depression.'[1]

It is by being assertive that we express who we are. To constantly set aside our rights can result in subconsciously failing to 'attack' difficult problems and make a mark. Along with such an opting out of life goes a buried angry feeling of being defeated, resentful, hurt and bitter. And that inward emotional experience of is, for many, the root of emotional illness. Repressed anger can simmer like a grumbling volcano — finally erupting with devastating personal results.

Often we back off and 'endure' because we see it is a far easier option than being assertive. It need not be. Personal skills can be brought into play that pitch a middle ground between acquiescence and blurting out, 'Blow smoke in my face once more and I'll nuke you into oblivion!'

Being assertive does not mean being selfish or self-centred. At times when we will choose not to be assertive through a desire to support and honour others or through a desire to help, no matter what the level of our personal inconvenience. But someone who constantly puts their own needs last has lost touch with reality. To do so sounds wonderfully gallant and sacrificial. In reality, others can end up picking up the pieces. Their pieces.

Feel better about yourself

The way we see ourselves — self-image — and the way we express ourselves to others — assertiveness — go hand in hand. Both hold a significant sway over our emotional wholeness and ability to manage our lives.

If you have a long-standing feeling of being unloved or unlovable you are particularly in danger of having a poor self image. Such a deep-seated feeling is likely to have its roots in your experiences in childhood which have conditioned your adult expectations. A parent who never expressed appreciation, said, 'Well done' or 'I'm proud of you' can leave an indelible mark. As can a constant flow of criticism and a sense that you were never quite good enough.

The end result is someone with a set of assumptions neatly categorised by Aaron Beck as follows:

- To be happy I must be accepted by all people at all times.
- If I make a mistake it means that I am inept.
- If someone disagrees with me, it means they do not like me.
- My value as a person depends on what others think of me.

Far too many people base their lives on this kind of wrong thinking. And it is those with such a distorted sense of reality that struggle most with assertiveness and so become trampled under foot. A compelling need to be accepted, liked and agreed with are all major motivators for us to keep our heads down rather than express our firm convictions or stand for our rights.

Become more comfortable with who you are. At any one moment there are four basic forces pulling at us. In every situation we have to come to terms with:

- what we believe we ought to be;
- what others expect us to be;
- what we really want to be;
- what we actually are.

This can represent an inner struggle of epic proportions. And when the stress this generates becomes greater than our own ability to maintain the balance, we are likely to contributing to our own stress overload.

The secret is to take time to set realistic goals for ourselves. And to build a picture of how God feels about us and what he expects from us. From such a position of security the expectation of others can be held at bay.

Keep things in perspective

Stress makes it very easy to lose perspective. Small problems can seem difficult and intimidating. Naturally this feeds your stress, making bad things worse. Don't let every irritation become the end of the world. It isn't.

Aim for a positive approach to life, looking for a good side to every situation. Faced with a seemingly overwhelming problem, ask yourself:

- Is this really a problem at all? Or is it more an opportunity to learn and triumph?
- Who else has been there before? Find out how they dealt with it.
- Can you break the problem down? How can you reduce this seemingly impossible problem to a number of smaller, more manageable tasks?
- Does it really matter anyway? If it matters now, will it matter in six months or a year? As long as you have done your best, and learned from any mistakes you make, then you cannot do any better.

Think positively

Negative thoughts are when you put yourself down, see yourself as inept, doubt your abilities and expect failure. Such thinking creates doubts in your mind that you are equal to the task you face. And that causes stress.

So track your thoughts for a while, perhaps when under stress. Look out for negative thoughts, no matter how fleeting. Are you worried about how you appear to other people? Constantly self-critical? Expressing feelings of inadequacy?

If so, write these thoughts down and consider them rationally. Do they have any basis in reality? Really. Now counter-attack with positive affirmations of your self to build confidence. Try phrases like:

- I can do this.
- I deserve to be liked for who I am.
- I am in control of my life.
- I learn from my mistakes. They increase the basis of experience on which I can draw.
- I am a good and valued person in my own right.
- My failures make me a more valuable person to others.

Accept your emotions

Studies show that those who are most vulnerable to stress are those who bottle up their emotions. Be warned: burying your anger, frustrations or hurts will only cause you harm. Talking to a friend or partner is a good way to let your emotions out.

The psalmist David is not the only one who expressed his anger and frustration to God. And God was far from being upset about it. Rather, he was so impressed he even arranged to include their stories in the Bible. Expressing your emotions to God, even those of hostility, is more acceptable than your guilty feelings would have you believe.

Studies also show that those who see crying as only for weak people are more likely to suffer from nervous illness. So be prepared to let it all out. Jesus wept and there are times when we should too. Incidentally, tears actually relieve stress by getting rid of potentially dangerous chemicals created in the body at stressful times.

Be forgiving

The apostle Paul's advice to 'settle your arguments before going to bed' has a sound psychological base. It 'fights' a situation that would otherwise remain unresolved and stress-inducing. The Christian concept of forgiveness walks the same road. Each act of reconciliation also ministers to our own physical and emotional well-being.

Cultivate a fixed sense of reality

One notable common theme comes from the advice given by stress counsellors and doctors. They point out that each of us needs 'something to believe in'. While few lay claim to a personal Christian faith, they still declare: 'Have a sense of belief'; 'Look for something to hold on to'; 'Develop a sense or purpose'.

Let me quote authors Walter McQuade and Ann Aikman from their wonderfully titled book *Stress: How to Stop your Mind Killing your Body*. Neither seems to make any claim to a personal Christian commitment. Yet they say, 'Religion in a devout believer has little equal as an allayer of stress. This is true of all religions, but particularly true of some. The Judaic-Christian tradition, for example, takes on all the primal stresses, and if it does not dispose of them completely it makes them surprisingly bearable.'[2]

More remarkably, they continue, 'the waning power of religion is one reason why life has become so stressful in the western world, and also why many people today are reconsidering and turning once again to religious faith, the more evangelical, it seems, the more popular.'[3]

These professionals recognise our need to hold change and threat at bay. Today the battle is great because we live under the shadow of the influence of philosophers like Jean-Paul Sartre and Søren Kierkegaard.

Have you ever heard the phrase, 'It doesn't matter what you believe as long as you are sincere'? Or, 'If it feels good, do it'? Then you have encountered the influence of Sartre's existentialism.

Without even realising it, the unspoken conviction of most of the Western world is that there is no longer any fixed 'truth' — each of us believes what is right or wrong 'for us'. Sincerity is what matters, while 'belief' is free to change from moment to moment. There is no longer a God who does not change. Only our individual experience counts — which may be different for each of us and alters constantly.

The intellectuals of our day have thrown away the idea that we can really 'know' anything in a rational sense. The emphasis is on experience. Unchanging and fixed values are out the window. Moral choices now depend not on truth but on circumstances. The world has been stood on its head. In the entertainment media, for example, villains are now held up as heroes. No wonder the advice is that we should find something, anything, to cling to.

It is at this point that I stand taller, confident in the relevance of having a commitment to God through his son Jesus Christ. Far from being knowable only through my inward experience, I can relate to a God who has made himself known in history, in Jesus and in the Bible. This personal God offers me a fixed point of reference in a changing world.

A significant weapon in the fight against stress is to develop a knowledge of and a relationship with the God who made us. Read about him in the Bible. Hear what others who know him have to say. Lock parts of the Bible away in your memory. Spend time using what you learn as a basis for quiet prayer and reflection.

Our security comes from knowing God's character and his purposes. Yet there is an even greater dimension to be gained when we move from merely knowing about God to actually knowing him in an intimate, loving and personal relationship.

It is one thing to know in theory that 'God is love.' It is quite another to experience personally the strength and warmth that God has for us.

Be thankful

Do not let past or future fears absorb your mind. Instead, focus on being grateful. Make a list of five or six things for which you can be truly thankful — no matter how trivial they may seem.

Carry the list with you; stick it on your mirror; write it on a postcard and send it to yourself; tuck it into your Bible. At every turn, use this simple method to help fight the lies that life is all bad being told by your emotions.

Being thankful includes recognising the positive value of your own sufferings. Be grateful that it will enable you to be more sympathetic and of greater help and value to others going through the mill.

Your grateful list

List here at least five things for which you are grateful, no matter what.

Then use the list — when things are bad — to remind you that its not always like that

1.

2.

3.

4.

5.

6.

Be determined

Whatever you do, hang on. The human spirit is more resilient than most of us give it credit for.

In those months when the dark clouds gathered, Rosemary would fill the house with the sound of Barbra Streisand belting out, 'I'll never give up.' She made it her song, translating its emotional content into her own experience just as far as she could.

Be realistic

Reduce your stress and pressure by choosing how you respond to the circumstances you face. Queuing for petrol or at a supermarket check-out provides the opportunity to fret, be anxious, constantly check the time, moan and generally boil over. None of which, incredibly, will cause the queue to move one bit faster.

Instead, we can choose to seize on this unexpected oasis as a moment to slow down, breathe deeply and relax.

Yes, I know this is glib and seemingly unrealistic when the whole world and its mother are screaming for your time from every direction. But the reality is that our attitude will not alter the way things are. As Jesus said, 'Who of you by worrying can add a single hour to his life?' (Matthew 6:27, NIV).

Some people come complete from the factory with an even

My action plan

In each space write something positive like:

- get a good night's sleep
- reduce the amount of caffeine I drink
- use deep breathing when stuck in traffic
- join a health club

And then do it!

To survive against stress I will:

Exercise — — — — — — — —

Rest — — — — — — — —

Food — — — — — — — —

Fun — — — — — — — —

Environment — — — — — — — —

Attitude — — — — — — — —

Relaxation — — — — — — — —

and placid temperament. Others, to quote Josh McDowell, 'stand in front of the microwave screaming, "Hurry!"' Yet every one of us can make a conscious choice to accept the unchangeable circumstances that confront us. As the well-known prayer goes, 'Lord, grant me the strength to change that which needs changing, the courage to accept that which cannot be changed, and the wisdom to know the difference.'

Trust in a God who acts

The God and Father of our Lord Jesus Christ is a God who is on our side. We pray — he listens and acts. He is concerned to work out his plans and purposes in our life. So, when neither 'fight' or 'flight' is possible, it helps to settle the matter by putting it into his trustworthy hands.

We reduce the toll of stress when we resolve our unresolved situations by letting God in on them. Sadly, we tend to reserve our prayers of 'Father, please take over' for moments of desperation. The secret is to learn to place the details of our lives into his capable and compassionate hands moment by moment.

Whatever the threat — or threats — and no matter what fear they create, the best place for them is in the care of an all-knowing and all-powerful heavenly Father. After all, 365 times in the Scriptures, Jesus said, 'Do not be afraid.' That is enough for every day.

8

I would often turn over in bed in the early hours to the smell of baking or new paint.

Sleepless in Suburbia

There is 'not being able to get to sleep' and 'not being able to get to sleep'. I have had first-hand encounters with both kinds.

Last night was one of the former. Through my mind raced a bunch of pressures, including the deadline for this book, some issues with two of our children's education, and a letter leading me to believe someone was spreading rumours which would significantly undermine my reputation as a consultant.

Throughout the night I wriggled, squirmed, and found — wicked or not — there was no rest to be had.

I 'awoke' feeling I'd never slept and wondering how I would make it through the day. But I know that tomorrow — or at least a day after — it will be back to normal. I will back to sleeping like a baby. Which seems a strange expression seeing that babies actually wake every three hours screaming their heads off. But you know what I mean.

Rosemary has experienced the other kind of 'can't sleep'. During her long and dark days — which had significant impact on her nights — I would often turn over in bed in the early hours to the smell of fresh baking or new paint.

She decided being unable to sleep for hours on end and nights in succession could at least be put to good use. As a result, all the Christmas cooking had been done by the end of August. And the house had never seen so much fresh paint.

Of course, we are not alone. Vast numbers of people have problems sleeping and the problem is growing.

Insomnia is the catch-all word used to cover sleeplessness problems including:

- difficulty falling asleep;
- waking up frequently during the night with difficulty returning to sleep;
- waking up too early in the morning;
- unrefreshing sleep.

In America they now talk of a national nightmare. According to the *Life* magazine.[1] There are now 3,000 Sleep Disorder Clinics to help address 'an epidemic of sleeplessness'. There is even a National Commission on Sleep Disorders, with goverment funding. The magazine claims that 'in 1910, Americans averaged nine hours of sleep per night. Today, its seven'.

Many now see the impact of nights without sleep for those who drive cars as being in the same category as drink-driving. Indeed, some notorious man-made disasters, including the 1989 Exxon Valdez oil spill, the nuclear leaks at Chernobyl and Three Mile Island and the Bhopal chemical catastrophe in India, occurred in the last hours before dawn, when even the most practised night worker has difficulty staying awake. These hours have become known as the zombie zone.

The *Life* article blames it all on the light bulb. This invention of Thomas Edison — a notorious short-sleeper — made it possible for shift work, longer daytime hours, evenings watching television and a whole bunch of other shenanigans. The rhythm of life changed and so did the rhythm of sleeping and waking.

Today — or should that be tonight? — the Edison legacy is vast and even stretches to a growing and seemingly endless number of TV channels, all-night shopping and the Internet. Two-thirds of the American work force now spend more than half their working life outside of the 'normal' 9 to 5 Monday to Friday working week. And the UK is following the trend.

The growing number of 'open all hours' telephone services involve not only the 200,000 who serve in them but those who stay up to use them. It is a wonder anyone ever has time to try to get to sleep.

Researchers claim that, while individual needs vary, about eight hours is the average sleep requirement. And teenagers need more than nine hours a night to keep themselves to maximum alertness — no matter what they may tell us.

In truth, an occasional restless night has no long term negative effect. But if night and day continually run into each other, and it starts to 'get to you' or affects the quality of your waking life and ability to function, you have a problem. And many people do.

Sleep problems can be found in both sexes and in all age groups. But they it seem to be more common in females — especially after menopause — and in the elderly. In most cases the core reason for difficulty in sleeping is emotional. Things like anxiety and internalised, unexpressed anger are common causes, as is depression.

Another common factor is when there is a big change in daily routine. For example, travelling, starting a new job, going into hospital or moving to a new home. This kind of problem usually doesn't last for more than a few days.

The word 'insomnia' actually covers all kinds of lack of sleep — from the occasional to the weeks-on-end variety. But it is chronic insomnia — the kind that does on and on — that creates the most pressure and needs the most help.

What can be done?

When all else fails, talk to your doctor — and take your medicine. But until then, here are 34 things to try other than counting sheep. They're all designed to help you deal with tension, stress and anxiety.

Not every one of these techniques by itself will get you to sleep, but a few of them at least should prove successful. For the best results, work at them over a period of time. You may need two to four weeks to see the best results.

Twenty-five things to do

1. Go to bed only when sleepy.
2. Use the bed only for sleeping — and that other thing.
3. If you can't sleep, get up and move to another room. Stay up until you feel sleepy and then return to bed. If sleep does not come get out of bed again. The aim is to associate your bed with falling asleep easily. Repeat this step as often as is necessary throughout the night.
4. Set the alarm and get up at the same time every morning, regardless of how much you have slept through the night.
5. Take some exercise in the late afternoon or early evening.
6. Drink herb tea.
7. Get a massage.
8. Try eating foods just before bed time that have tryptophan — like turkey and bananas.
9. Sleep on a good firm bed.
10. Sleep on your back.
11. Don't sleep in.
12. Spend 20 minutes in a hot bath not long before going to bed.
13. Keep the room temperature as constant as you can.
14. Eat a light bedtime snack.
15. Drink a glass of warm milk — as milk contains an amino acid that converts to a sleep-enhancing compound in the brain.
16. Make love.
17. Use simple relaxation and mind clearing exercises.
18. Keep a note pad by the bed to write down things that come to mind that you worry you might forget.
19. Try to break the cycle by deliberately staying awake for an whole night.
20. Go to bed at the same time each day.
21. Get up at the same time each day.
22. Get regular exercise each day.

23. Keep the bedroom quiet when sleeping.
24. Keep the bedroom dark enough. Use dark blinds or wear an eye mask if needed.
25. When you go to bed, relax your muscles, beginning with your feet and working your way up to your head.

Nine things not to do

1. Don't exercise just before going to bed.
2. Do not nap excessively during the daytime.
3. Avoid 'trying to sleep'.
4. Avoid illuminated bedroom clocks.
5. Don't stimulate your mind just before bed through things like playing a competitive game of cards or watching an exciting TV programme.
6. Avoid caffeine. Remember that caffeine is present in chocolate, as well as regular coffee or tea, and caffeinated soft drinks.
7. Don't read or watch television in bed.
8. Don't use alcohol to help you sleep.
9. Don't take another person's sleeping pills.

If all this fails, the question is bound to come 'what about sleeping pills?' This medical help is mainly used to treat the short-lasting insomnia that can impact us following a bereavement or other major change. The rules are simple. If sleeping pills are prescribed use them only as directed. And expect to use them for no more than two weeks, because after that they may actually make the problem worse.

This means that you should never depend on sleeping pills alone to solve your problem. Alongside your medication must go a serious attempt at stress management. And, as you have seen, this is nothing to lose sleep over.

9

Once when two cars collided their drivers exchanged insurance details. Now, they are as likely to exchange blows.

Car fumes

It happens to everyone: you're backed up in traffic, trying to get through town. Every light turns red just as you get there. A journey timed for 10 minutes stretches to 30. You finally arrive, you're late, frazzled, and practically asphyxiated from exhaust fumes.

The other drivers have not helped your mental state. What happened to old-fashioned courtesy? Why do so many selfish people take advantage by charging down the outside lane when it is about to merge with yours? Why is the one direction sign you need always the one missing?

The truth is, driving is no longer fun. And it hasn't been for a very long time. Should you dare to disagree I will pull rank. After all, I live within a horn's toot of the M25.

What I have described is having an impact. Once upon a time, when two cars collided their drivers politely exchanged insurance details. Now, they are as likely to exchange blows. At least they will be if the current trend in what has become known as 'road rage' continues.

America, of course, has more cars, more drives, more 'road rage' But the UK is fast catching up. How long before incidents like the following two become part of our way of life as well?

February, 1994. Two drivers became embroiled in a heated, on-going traffic dispute. Having antagonised each other for several miles on a major Massachusetts highway, the two men pulled over and got out of their vehicles. At that point, one of them — a 54-year old book keeper — took a powerful crossbow from his boot and murdered the other with a razor-sharp 29-inch arrow.

August, 1995. A prominent lawyer was driving his sons to see his ailing father in hospital. Suddenly his 1990 Jeep Cherokee bumped into a newer model whose driver was six months pregnant. The lawyer, later described as seeming to be 'out of control', struck the mother-to-be in the face, breaking her sunglasses and giving her a black eye that lasted for ten days. This bastion of the establishment was convicted of battery and malicious destruction of property.

So serious has the road rage become in the US that it has been the subject of considerable research.[1] This reveals at least 1,500 people injured or killed each year there as a result of aggressive driving'. And, over the last recorded seven year period, at least 10,000 incidents of aggressive driving.

The most common road rage experiences of drivers were:

- aggressive tailgating — 6 out of 10;
- headlight flashing — 6 out of 10;
- obscene gestures — 1 in 2;
- deliberately obstructing other vehicles — 1 in 5;
- verbal abuse — 1 in 6.

As a direct result of all this:

- at least 218 people were murdered;
- 12,610 people suffered injuries including paralysis, brain damage and amputation.

So which maladjusted psychopaths are responsible for all this mayhem? The data indicates no distinct profile of the so-called 'aggressive driver' in terms of age and background. However, many have previously suffered an emotional or professional set-back, or suffered an injury or an accident. Yet hundreds of aggressive drivers — motorists who have cracked and committed incredible violence — are successful people with no known history of crime or violence. When the media interview their friends and neighbour the message is 'he is the nicest man', 'a wonderful father', or 'he must have been provoked'.

But that is America. What about us? In 1995, research by the AA's Road Safety Unit[2] found that of those drivers surveyed over the previous twelve months:

- nine out of ten had experienced 'road rage' incidents;
- three in five admitted to losing their tempers behind the wheel;
- one in every hundred claimed they had been physically assaulted by another motorist.

Further research, two years later, created a fuller picture. This survey of more than one thousand people was part of Cornhill Insurance's[3] campaign to emphasise to the public the result of increased motor insurance premiums to those convicted of aggressive driving.

The big story was the nearly one in four of adults revealed to have committed an act of road rage, with men almost three times more likely to offend than women.

Also in on the act were Lex Vehicle Leasing[4], with a survey revealing drivers now feel more vulnerable at the wheel than every before. The company called for the setting up of a road rage hotline. The plea was based on the statistic that over the previous twelve months, over two million people had been road rage victims — with over a half having been forced to pull over or off the road. While 130,000 had actually been attacked by other drivers.

The Cornhill Research includes a telling statement that four out of five people believe a person's character changes for the worst when they get behind the wheel — and people are being killed or injured as a result.

Though the term 'road rage' can refer to any aggression by a driver it tends to be reserved for more extreme acts of aggression that occur as a direct result of a disagreement between drivers.

There is nothing to suggest that road rage is distinct from any other form of anger. But for many people, driving is now one of the most frustrating activities they are regularly engaged in.

Surviving 'road rage'

Do not become a victim. If you feel threatened by another motorist, here's how to defuse the situation or protect yourself:

- Try not to react.

- Avoid making eye contact, which can seem confrontational.

- Don't be tempted to accelerate, brake, or swerve suddenly — this may be seen as confrontational and increases your chances of losing control of your vehicle.

- If a driver continues to hassle you or you think you are being followed, drive to the nearest police station or busy place to get help.

- In town, lock the car doors and keep the windows and sunroof only partly open.

- When stopped in traffic, leave enough space to pull out from behind the car you are following.

- If someone tries to get into your car, attract attention by sounding your horn and switching on the hazard lights.

Having defined the problem, it is time to address it. First, there is the need to minimise your own stress as you drive. Here's how:

- Always anticipate congestion, whether the journey is two or twenty miles. So allow ten minutes for what would normally be a five minute trip. And thirty minutes for a longer motorway journey.

- Double-check the journey route before you leave and plan an escape route just in case.

- Choose to give the other driver the benefit of the doubt.

- Remember to take a road map with you — always.

- Assume that, however poorly other drivers may perform, their mistakes are not on purpose and not personally aimed at you.

- Do some 'seat aerobics' — tensing muscles and releasing them.

- Before blowing up at another driver's gaffe, ask yourself, 'How many times have I done the same?'

- Adjust your car seat: shoulders should be relaxed, arms slightly bent and head upright.

- Don't sit too straight up as the neck muscles have to work harder to support your head.

- Don't grip the wheel too tightly, as this tenses the muscles.

- Never drive when you are angry, upset or over-tired.

- Keep the car cool; overheating causes drowsiness and loss of concentration.

- Take a short break after driving for two hours. This helps circulation and keeps the mind alert.

- Ask yourself, 'Is it really the end of the world if I am a bit late'?

- Get fit. A poor diet and lack of exercise means being less fit to drive.

- Always remember that while you can't control the traffic, you can control your reaction to it.

Children must be one of great stress-inducers on any journey. And not just because of the constant cries of 'Are we nearly there yet?' Books, audio tapes, felt tip pens are all part of the parent's survival kit. But at times you will need more. Perhaps our two family 'keep them amused' games may just work for yours.

The one ours have liked best is 'Car Bingo'. The winner is the first to spot about five pre-agreed items like — a police car, an AA van, a car with its bonnet up, any three different kinds of animal, a car towing a boat. Those who have already spotted a particular category still try to spot it first to stop the others claiming it as theirs. We also throw in a wild card — something like a tractor — which can count for any item.

The one Rosemary and I enjoy most is 'Guess How Long?'. You will understand why. Pick an object a long way in the distance — a bridge, or a building, or whatever. All the passengers close their eyes and say when they think they have reached it, with some significant word like 'Now'. The one closest wins. This is a wonderfully quiet game for a manic journey.

Finally there is something somewhat ironic about this chapter. Some of the information comes courtesy of Vauxhall Cars who have been advertising their Omega range with the theme 'a car that helps you relax'. They even sponsored a series of supplements on stress in a major Sunday newspaper — taking the high ground in terms of their contribution to over-stressed drivers.

The irony is that I actually have owned an Omega — which has caused me more stress than any car I have ever driven. Among many other things, it has an automatic immobilising system — probably now modified — which has left us stranded in a variety of remote locations. And has the a horn on the outer perimeter of the steering wheel. So that whenever you need it you can never find it — unless the car happens to be pointing absolutely straight forward at the time.

All this means that the time is coming soon when I look forward to reducing my own driving stress — by trading in my Omega for something else.

10

Almost every job in Britain today is more stressful than a decade ago — with the stress levels of many now rated as worryingly high.

Workers' stress-time

With a spring in their step those Seven Dwarfs waltzed their way to work. In stark contrast, many of us today head for the daily grind muttering, 'I owe, I owe, it's off to work I go.' And the last thing on our mind is whistling a happy tune.

Something bad is happening in the workplace. Every day in the UK, some 270,000 people take time off because of stress-related illness. That means 40 million working days lost each year — stinging employers for between £7 and £9 billion in sick pay, missed deadlines and poor performance.[1]

But before looking at why this should be and what we can do, note that not all jobs generate the same levels of stress. The University of Manchester Institute of Science and Technology has completed a study categorising the jobs likely to produce the greatest stress.[2] In the list on the next page, the rating is from 0 to 10. The higher the number, the greater the stress:

Stress at work

Prison officer	8.8	Marketing/export	5.2
Police officer	8.7	Solicitor	5.0
Social worker	8.5	Civil servant	4.8
Teacher	8.3	Engineer	4.8
Nurse/midwife	8.2	Estate agent	4.8
Doctor	8.0	Postal carrier	4.8
Dentist	7.7	Psychologist	4.8
Fireman	7.7	Publishing	4.8
Miner	7.7	Vet	4.8
Armed forces	7.5	Accountant	4.7
Construction worker	7.2	Banker	4.5
Manager (commerce)	7.0	Computer operator	4.5
Actor	7.0	Planner	4.5
Film producer	6.8	Nursery worker	4.3
Journalist	6.8	Statistician	4.3
Linguist	6.8	Art & design	4.2
Professional footballer	6.7	Architect	4.0
Advertising	6.5	Chiropodist	3.8
Bus driver	6.5	Minister	3.7
Farmer	6.3	Optician	3.7
Local government officer	6.3	Hairdresser	3.5
Pilot	6.3	Lab technician	3.5
Stockbroker	6.3	Librarian	3.3
Personnel	5.7	Museum worker	3.3
Musician	5.5	Beauty therapist	2.5
Secretary	5.5	Astronomer	2.3
Occupational therapist	5.3		

The reasons for one job carrying more stress than another vary considerably. Dentists dislike being treated as inflictors of pain — which helps to explain their suicide rate of twice the national average. Pop musicians and actors face stress from financial insecurity, performance nerves and their own self-criticism. Construction workers, have stress inflicted on them through noise on the job.

Rosemary wondered whether a home-maker — or domestic engineer, as she once described herself — qualifies for an accumulation of stress factors relating to all the jobs they do. She lists them as including politician, doctor, nurse/midwife, teacher, social worker, manager, psychologist, diplomat, accountant and nursery worker. The average rating of those jobs would put her in the top half of the stress bracket just above stock brokers and just below salesmen. The husband who arrives home in the evening and asks cheerily, 'What have you been doing all day?' deserves all he gets.

Fight for survival

There is something additionally significant about these statistics. The survey, conducted in 1997, followed on from an identical study twelve years earlier. Simple comparison shows almost every job in Britain as more stressful today than a decade ago — with the stress levels of many now rated as worryingly high. Over that time more than six out of ten of the more than 100 jobs assessed showed increases in levels of stress.

The lesson from all this is that when it comes to the rat race, the rats are winning. Grandad learnt a skill for life. Dad climbed the corporate ladder to comfort and security. But we now fight for survival. It is not hard to understand why this is, in view of the revolution taking place in the workplace. Consider the following:

Changing work patterns. On the way out are the nine to five workdays, lifetime jobs, predictable, hierarchical relationships, corporate cultural security blankets, and, for a large and growing sector of the workforce, the workplace itself.

What stresses you at work?

Research on 1,000 managers in ten countries identified their top twelve stressors as:

- time pressures and deadlines
- work overload
- inadequately trained subordinates
- long working hours
- attending meetings
- demands of work on private and social life
- keeping up with new technology
- holding beliefs that conflict with those of the organisation
- taking work home
- lack of power and influence
- the amount of travel required by work
- doing a job below one's level of competence

And here are some more they did not mention:

- too much or too little work
- having to perform outside of your experience or ability
- having to overcome unnecessary obstacles
- unrealistic time pressures and deadlines
- keeping up with procedures and policies
- lack of relevant support and advice
- lack of clear goals
- under-promotion, frustration and boredom
- lack of a clear plan for career development
- lack of opportunity
- lack of job security
- demands from clients

In particular, people are having to adjust to the disappearance of jobs for life. Work is no longer the stable environment it once was. Indeed:

- A survey in 1994 revealed that nearly one in six UK employees had been in their present job for less than a year, and half for less than five years.[3]
- The number of self-employed workers in the UK has increased from just over 2 million in 1971 to almost 3.4 million in 1994 — an increase of almost 70 per cent.[4]

Previous generations expected a minimum number of moves within their career lifetime. The parting handshake, accompanied by a gold watch for twenty-five years of faithful service, was not the rare event it is today. Employment offering that kind of security is becoming increasingly difficult to find. Even long-term employees are regularly shuffled and redistributed to new tasks and locations.

Those entering the world of work today face a prospect of being retrained three times before retiring, with job-hopping, and even career-hopping as the standard way life works. Others are working on the new vogue of limited contract commitment where, either as an individual specialist or part of a specially-recruited team, they work on a short-term project before moving on to new people and environments to start again.

In particular, the overwhelming trend is towards work which is temporary or part-time. This is sometimes because that's the way people want to work. More often because that is all that's available.

Longer working hours. Until the late 1980s there was a constant trend towards the length of the working week becoming shorter and shorter for the average Briton. All has changed. In the 1990s, people in jobs have rarely worked harder or longer. Now:

- The average employee in Britain works almost 45 hours a week, longer than any equivalent nation in the European Union.
- One in four of British male employees work more than 48

hours a week, one in five manual workers work more than 50 hours a week and one in eight British managers works more than 60 hours a week.

- In the past ten years the number of people working 50 hours or more a week has risen to more than one in five of the workforce — an increase of 40 per cent.
- The average British lunch hour is now 30 minutes.
- Seven out of ten British workers want to work only 40 hours a week but only three out of ten do so.
- More than one in ten out of the workforce — almost 2.5 million people, have no annual paid leave.

Greater pressure. The jargon word is 'downsizing'. Which being interpreted meaneth fewer people will now do just as much or even more with less resources and support. That's the reason for the longer hours. And also for the new business culture where:

- even if there is nothing to do, no one dare be the first to leave at night — and the one who turns the lights out gets the brownie points.
- some are even afraid to use their holiday entitlement. They may need the money in lieu should their job go — or find they haven't been missed while away and so discover their job is at risk.

Information overload. Today's technology makes generating and storing large quantities of information easier than ever before. Just as the steam engine and the invention of electricity brought about the industrial revolution, so the information revolution has been fuelled by the development of the integrated circuit. This amazing technology, invented only in the late 1950s, permits ever-increasing volumes of information to be processed or stored on a single micro-chip.

As a result, more information has been produced in the past 30 years than during the previous 5,000. Indeed, a weekday edition of *The Times* contains more information than the average person was likely to come across in a lifetime during seventeenth century England.

More than that, the deluge keeps coming. Twenty-five years ago, there were fewer than 25,000 computers on the planet. Today there are more than 200 million. The information supply doubles every five years. All of which impacts the workplace environment, accelerated by e-mail and the Internet.

A study, Communications Overload, by Gallup and the Institute for the Future[5] found that:

- the average middle-management executive sends or receives 178 messages and documents each day;
- secretarial staff face more than 190 daily correspondences, including post, e-mail, faxes, phone calls, voice-mail, sticky notes, pager messages, courier deliveries and Internet mail;
- more than seven out of ten managers feel overwhelmed by their correspondence.

All this is a significant cause of stress, ill-health and poor quality of life. And don't take my word for it. An independent,

---

How to fight information overload

Here are a few ways to keep from drowning in the lake of information overload.

- Accept the fact that you can't know everything.

- Prioritise — by deciding which of your messages you're even going to bother reading, opening or checking.

- Separate the important from the merely urgent.

- Find ways to unsubscribe from mailing lists and circulars.

- Deal with information only once. Either respond, file or bin/ delete it.

international survey, 'Dying for information?',[6] published by Reuters Business Information, leaves no doubt this excess of information causes widespread mental anguish and physical illness.

The report coined the term Information Fatigue Syndrome, defining its symptoms as including:

- a hyper-aroused psychological condition
- paralysis of analytical capacity
- anxiety and self-doubt.

All of which led to:

- foolish decisions and flawed conclusions.

More specifically, the report reveals that due to the stress associated with information overload:

- Two thirds of managers say it leads to tension with work colleagues and loss of job satisfaction.
- One in every six executives and managers suffer from depression or critical levels of stress.
- One third suffer from ill-health.
- Half predict the Internet will only make thing worse.

What can be done in the battle to survive in the workplace? Try the following for starters.

See where God fits in. The right perspective will take you a long way. Work is not a punishment for the disobedience of our first ancestors. It was part of God's plan from the very beginning. Remember, work is God's idea. He works and we are made in his image and work too.

However, it is true that sin and selfishness has made work into toil. Not least because of the selfishness and sin ruling the world in which we now work. If only everyone were perfect, think how easy our job would be. Nevertheless, work is not something we do in between serving God. It *is* serving God — every bit as much as those who spend their working lives on church stuff.

So among all the stress, remember your loving Father in heaven is glad you are there and wants it to be an experience where you serve him with all your mind and strength.

Be realistic. When stuck in the environment where you are constantly being asked to achieve more and more with less resources:

Pace yourself. It is better to work to a regular schedule — even if it involves extra long days — rather than solving the problem through big-bash around the clock efforts.

Cherish yourself. The right foods, and exercise are better than junk food, alcohol and nothing other than work to get your heart pumping.

Get real. Remember that those you report to know what they've done to your staff, budget and expectations. They only have the right to expect what is reasonable rather than to end up congratulating themselves for getting blood out of a stone.

Increase your feelings of self-worth. You will feel better about what you are doing if you can find a way to know, observe and be involved in the outcome of your efforts.

Work smart. Carve out at least one or two hours a day when you are not accepting calls or interruptions. By telling people when you will be available it helps keep them off your back.

Improve the air quality. You could: ban smoking; open windows; use an ioniser — to eliminate positive ions created, for example, by electric motors, powering computer fans; use dehumidifiers where humidity may be a problem. Introducing plants will raise the amount of oxygen in the air and reduce stuffiness.

See the light. Eye strain and increased fatigue, can be the result of lighting that is too dull, too bright, or that shines into your eyes. Fluorescent light can have the same impact. Fight for a place by a window or use full spectrum bulbs in your desk lamp.

Tidy up. Attack mess and disorder in your working environment. But if you are not naturally an 'everything in its place' person, don't inflict the pressure on yourself of trying to behave as though you are.

Turn down noise. Lessen the noise of your environment. Office noise creates tension that uses up 20 per cent of our energy, affecting ability to concentrate and creating irritability, tension and headaches.

Wherever possible, install partitions and sound absorbing soft furnishings; use a separate room for meetings and, when you need to concentrate, try earplugs.

Be comfortable. Arrange your working environment so it is comfortable. For example, the way you sit and what you sit on can create stress through muscular tension and pain. Make sure your chair has a firm back support.

If you use a computer, see that the monitor and keyboard are correctly positioned; consider using a 'natural' keyboard; try taking breaks periodically.

Build good relationships. Harmony with others helps fend off stress. Remember, people enjoy working with happy, optimistic people. A smile and a positive attitude can make the real difference. Take extra care over personal grooming. Learn about body language and the need to adopt a good, open posture. And remember to pay compliments when they are due.

Be positive. Your attitude is a key factor to long term stress management. By being negative or hostile, you will alienate

---

Beat burn-out

If you see yourself as a candidate for burning out, take action:

- Set more realistic goals and priorities.

- Reduce your commitments.

- If you face demands for too much of your emotional energy, step back and involve others in a supportive role. Be sure to avoid being bled dry emotionally.

- Start to use stress management skills — relaxation and breathing methods.

- Reduce the stress in your life.

- Get the support of your friends and family.

- Add 'fun' to your routine.

---

and irritate others. Yet with a positive attitude, you can maintain a sense of perspective and draw the positive elements out of every situation. And people will be more helpful and co-operative as they find you a pleasure to work with.

Accept change. The present information revolution and general workplace upheaval means that unless you learn to welcome change you will expose yourself to intense stress. Try to see change as a door to new opportunities.

Set goals. The most satisfying and enjoyable work you do may be the work you choose in pursuit of your own long term goals. So make sure you have some — and are working on them.

Be alert to burn-out. One of the worse aspects of the overload of stress is burn-out, which is not a scientific term, but a loose way to describe the experience of total mental and spiritual exhaustion. This is a land I have visited twice. And the landscape is far from inviting.

Day by day you simply feel utterly tuckered out. Energy, enthusiasm, and future-focus have gone. Stress symptoms abound — like dry mouth, itchy eyes, sweats, twitches and rashes. You drag yourself through the day, shuffling piles of paper and spending longer and longer achieving less and less.

Potential burn out victims are not hard to spot. They tend to be hard working, hard driven people who have been under intense and sustained pressure for some time. They are those who:

- find it difficult to say 'no' to additional commitments or responsibilities;
- have high standards that make it difficult to delegate;
- have been trying to achieve too much for too long;
- have been giving too much emotional support to others for too long.

Burn-out normally builds up slowly, over a long period of time. Look for early warning signals. Are you too busy? Is what you are doing no longer fun? Are you saying 'yes' when it should be 'no'?

Get drastic. One in four executives and managers are likely to agree with the statement, 'I would be willing to take a lower-paid job if it meant less stress and more free time'. And it can be done. There is a happy world out there, waiting for those willing to downsize their own expectations as to how much money they really need to live on and how much of the world they want to gain in exchange for their own soul.

This idea used to go by the somewhat complicated term 'voluntary simplicity'. Now it's called 'downshifting' — a move out of the rat race and into the human race. It is, at heart, a way to say, 'I will live on less and demand less of myself in exchange for a more peaceable, less frenetic lifestyle.'

It sounds remarkably like the way we would live if we took the teachings of Jesus seriously. Now there is an original idea.

11

So many despairing, frightened young people need help and counselling — and lots of love.

Growing up with stress

Seumas Todd took his own life after one year at university. The 20–year old student at Northumbria University left a suicide note saying he could not cope with the challenges and difficulties ahead.

Seumas' father, British actor Richard Todd, said afterwards, 'We have been made more than ever aware of the pressures youth faces nowadays, in the home, in school, in the university and particularly when embarking on the daunting, turbulent journey into a competitive world.'[1]

Richard Todd now knows from bitter personal experience the price of stress in student life. From a more detached view, Brian Thorn, of the University Counselling Services, asserts, 'The demand for student counselling has never been higher.' Indeed, about one in five students now consult a counsellor at their university each year.

From his intimate perspective, Richard Todd pinpoints some of the reasons for all this personal pain. He cites the fact so many more young people now go on into further education. As a result, government grants continue to fall short of what is needed for students to fend for themselves.

This and other factors have brought a situation where many:

- are forced to live miserably and unhealthily on very short rations;
- run into debts and overdrafts, spurred on by the current system of student loans;
- struggle to keep up with the academic schedule;
- have never been parted from their parents before and find the experience bewildering;
- toil away with the certain knowledge that a degree is no longer a reasonable guarantee at gaining a job at any level.

The impact of stress on university students has a link, without doubt, to the growing levels of stress and depression among adolescents. Recent surveys show as many as one in five teens suffer from clinical depression. One survey named stress and nervousness as the number one emotional problem felt by 14- to 21-year olds.

Teenage years are stressful enough without any 'help' from the world outside. The body grows more rapidly during puberty than any time outside of infancy. The mind and emotions are growing and changing too. There's a lot of stress in wondering 'What's happening to me?', 'Am I OK?', 'Am I as good as my friends?', or 'How can I go out with this zit on my nose?'

But being sure of yourself is not enough. Teens also need to feel sure of their friends. Yet teens grow and change, friendships and interests change too. It hurts when an old friend falls away or betrays your confidence.

Then there is the conflict involved in pushing boundaries and finding out which of several alternative personalities is really them. And the times when teens and parents clash — tell me about it!

Unrealistic academic, social, or family expectations can create a strong sense of rejection and lead to deep disappointment. When things go wrong at school or at home, teens often overreact. Many feel life is not fair or that things 'never go their way'.

To make matters worse, teens are bombarded by conflicting

messages from parents, friends and society. They see more of what life has to offer — both good and bad — on television, at school, in magazines and on the Internet. They are also forced to learn about the threat of AIDS, even if they are not sexually active or using drugs.

Family values

Teens face an added stress load if their family environment is one where Christian values are to the fore. They need to test their boundaries; are likely to have peers to whom this is Christian stuff all somewhat out of the ark and most likely they don't want to mess up their respectable parent's reputation. All this is a bunch of extra pressure they could do without and which certainly deserves some understanding.

The fact is that kids of Christian parents *do* mess up. My own five have all managed to do the things that 'normal' teenagers do during the perilous journey to adulthood. Between them — and the offspring of my Christian peers — they have managed to be found vomiting in the church carpark after an alcoholic binge, inflate a condom and let it off in class, be arrested in possession of cannabis, flattened a dinner supervisor and a few other things beside. But that's kids. Or at least it is the normal, healthy, out-going kind who will make their mark in the world.

At the very least 'What will people think?' is *not* the appropriate thing for a parent to say in the face of a serious episode of copy-book blotting like that. What teens need to know is while all else is changing, our love for them and commitment to them remains firm. And that our own reputation and inner security do not depend on them making a considerably better fist of their teenage years than we probably did.

When it all becomes too much, warning signs appear that may indicate depression — particularly when they last for more than two weeks. The symptoms include:

- poor performance in school;
- withdrawal from friends and activities;
- sadness and hopelessness;
- lack of enthusiasm, energy or motivation;
- anger and rage;
- overreaction to criticism;
- feelings of being unable to satisfy ideals;
- poor self-esteem or guilt;
- indecision, lack of concentration or forgetfulness;
- restlessness and agitation;
- changes in eating or sleeping patterns;
- substance abuse;
- problems with authority.

Teens may also experiment with drugs or alcohol or become sexually promiscuous to avoid feelings of depression. And may express their depression through hostile, aggressive, risk-taking behaviour.

Occasionally, teenage depression leads to an attempt at suicide. Encouragingly, four out of five teens who attempt such an extreme act give clear warnings. Sometimes the signs look like teenage normality. But are they really what you would expect of 'this' teen? The signs include:

- a dramatic change in their personality or appearance;
- irrational, bizarre behaviour;
- an overwhelming sense of guilt, shame or rejection;
- changed eating or sleeping patterns;
- a severe drop in school performance;
- giving away belongings.

And some signs should certainly stick out:

- suicide threats, direct and indirect;
- obsession with death;
- poems, essays and drawings that refer to death.

These warning signs are to be taken seriously. Teens need adult guidance more than ever to understand all the emotional and physical changes they are experiencing. They also have to know they are loved and accepted — no matter what.

When teens feel down, there are ways to help them avoid serious depression. All of the following strategies will help develop a sense of acceptance and belonging that is so important to adolescents. They should:

Try to make new friends. Healthy relationships with their peers are central to teens' self-esteem and provide an important social outlet.

Participate in sports, job, school activities or hobbies. Staying busy helps teens focus on positive activities rather than negative feelings or behaviour.

Join organisations with programmes for young people. Special programmes geared to the needs of adolescents help develop additional interests.

Ask a trusted adult for help. When problems are too much to handle alone, teens should not be afraid to ask for help.

Adoloescent depression

Sometimes, despite everyone's best efforts, teens become depressed. And adolescent depression is increasing at an alarming rate. This is a serious problem calling for a prompt and appropriate response. Depression is serious. Left untreated it can become life-threatening.

However, few adolescents seek help on their own. They may need encouragement from friends, and support from concerned adults to seek help and follow treatment recommendations.

Some of the most common and effective ways to treat depression in adolescents are:

Psychotherapy. This gives teens an opportunity to explore events and feelings that they find painful or troubling to them. Psychotherapy also teaches them coping skills.

Cognitive-behavioral therapy. This helps teens change negative patterns of thinking and behaving.

Interpersonal therapy. This focuses on how to develop healthier relationships at home and at school.

Medication. This relieves some symptoms of depression and is often prescribed along with therapy.

Richard Todd adds, 'We have had an astonishing number of letters from people whose children have taken their own lives in recent years. So many despairing, frightened young people need help and counselling — and lots of love.'

Certainly a radical re-think — and some positive action — has to be a priority if we are to stave off the emotional trauma already hitting today's students. On this front there is a great deal the local community — particularly churches — can do. A programme of hospitality, care, support and 'surrogate parenting' will go a very long way to helping more of them survive.

The part you can play is to offer help and a listening ear; to encourage depressed teens to talk about their feelings; and to listen rather than lecture. Trust your instincts. If it seems the situation may be serious, seek prompt help. Break a confidence if it means you may save a life.

But don't carry the burden all by yourself. If need be, seek expert advice from a mental health professional who has experience helping depressed teens. Also, alert those who are the key adults in the teen's life — family, friends and teachers.

When adolescents are depressed, they have a tough time believing their outlook can improve. But professional treatment can have a dramatic impact on their lives. It can put them back on track and bring them hope for the future.

*If we believe the lie that
Christians do not have
problems, we are going to
be inflicted with the stress
of guilt when reality strikes.*

12

Church — the
time for truth

Perhaps the greatest pressure point for those who follow Jesus
Christ is the assumption we are expected to cope with whatever life throws at us. That no matter how often or how
severely life takes an unkind turn, we will smile on through
and be quite immune to the pain of it all.

To quote the Sunday School song of a generation or two
ago, 'When Jesus Christ came in, he took away my sin. And
I'm in-right, out-right, up-right, down-right happy ALL the
time'. That's the expectation we can too often make of ourselves and even impose on others. And it is not hard to understand why.

It has been said that there are 'liars, damned liars and
politicians'. True or not, there are probably more lies told in
the ten minutes after a Sunday service in most of our churches
than in a whole week within the hallowed Palace of Westmin-
ster. Listen in with me to the all too typical 'Sunday lie-in':

'Hello Barbara, how are you?'

'Fine, Julie, fine. And how are you?'

'Fine. And you, Tom?'

'Fine. Just fine. How are you this morning, Stephen?'

'Oh, fine. Really fine.'

Now let's listen again and add what may really have been
going on in the minds of those involved.

'Hello, Barbara, how are you?' *(Must dash to get the lunch on.)*

'Fine, Julie, fine.' *(Except for three sleepless nights with baby James, a blazing row with Mike — again — and a panic attack in Sainsbury's.)* 'And how are you?'

'Fine.' *(Thank goodness she doesn't know what I'm really thinking. She'd have a fit.)* 'And you, Tom?'

'Fine. Just fine.' *(If I told her even half, it would be around this place faster than head lice at a nursery school.)* 'How are you, Stephen?'

'Oh, fine. Really fine.' *(If you really care, where have you been all week while life has been kicking me in the teeth? Anyway, didn't I drop you enough hints last time you asked this meaningless question?)*

We have even become so preconditioned to the anticipated answer that even telling the truth does not always solve the problem. On the church steps, dropping my children off to their activities I have responded to a 'How are you?' with 'Pretty desperate.' Only to receive a smile and the reply, 'Praise the Lord!'

Rosemary remembers receiving a phone call from a very dear friend concerned to see how she was while I was away for several days. Having blurted out how difficult things had been and how bad she was feeling, Rosemary paused for breath — only to hear the caller come back with the pre-programmed reply, 'Oh, good!'

There are ways to break the mould. We discovered the perfect unnerving reply to the 'How are you?' question is, 'Just about the same'. This produces a wonderful disorientation when people realise they ought to know how you were the last time they asked!

A more positive approach is to reply, 'That's a big question. If you really want to know, call in for coffee and I will tell you.' That method will probably not bring floods of people to your door. The reason is simple: 'How are you?' really means nothing more significant than 'Good morning'. So the lies being told in church have as much to do with the question as they do with the answers. We don't really want to know how people are because an honest answer has implications for us that we may want to avoid.

This is not a new phenomenon. The apostle Paul had to tell the early Christians to 'carry each other's burdens' (Galatians 6:2, NIV). If it had been happening naturally within the church, he wouldn't have needed to give the command.

Leadership conspiricy

The Sunday 'cover up' is not limited to the casual conversations after the service. It is equally present in the pulpit. Can you remember the last time you heard the preacher honestly share their own problems, needs, hurts or failings — if ever? Here is a 'role model' that we are likely to take on board. If the minister, the example of 'true spirituality', never has problems, then obviously we shouldn't either. We become victims of their conspiracy of silence.

A psychiatrist conducted a random telephone survey of a hundred American clergymen selected from various denominations. One in five clergymen revealed they had experienced moderate to severe depression at some time in their life. There is every reason to believe that a similar survey conducted in Britain would bring similar results. Yet how often do we hear that truth revealed publicly from the ministers themselves?

Dishonesty at leadership level is a major burden inflicted on everyone else. One of my favourite cartoons comes from an American Christian leadership publication. A wife is applying a clothes brush to the jacket of her minister husband as he is about to leave home for church. She is saying, 'Suppose you do it the other way around for a change today, dear. Be nice at home and ratty at church.'

That kind of honesty is essential if we are to lift unrealistic burdens from the shoulders of hurting people. We need those at leadership level who are not only willing to open up the Bible, but also to open up themselves. Otherwise, the minister's study can easily become a refuge from reality, and 'professionalism' an escape from humanness.

If we swallow the lie that Christians do not have problems, we are going to be inflicted with the stress of guilt when reality strikes. Instead of looking for help or being honest about how things are with us, we will struggle along — fallen and defeated.

No problems

This is a terrible burden for people to bear. Rosemary discovered that to her cost. Everything within the environment of our church proclaimed, 'Christians do not have problems'. As a result, she could not bring herself to admit she was taking anti-depressants. It was almost three months before I knew the truth.

Rosemary felt so guilty at having problems and not being able to cope. Everywhere else, people with bigger hills to climb were saying, 'Fine, I'm fine,' smiling and getting by. So she told herself she ought to be able to manage with her own resources.

The ultimate crunch came when I answered my office telephone to hear Rosemary's distressed voice. I wasn't unduly surprised, because the children had been playing up of late and, to top it all, her cloud of depression had not shifted for days. But all this was not the cause of her distress.

I learned that earlier in the day a loyal and well-meaning friend had stopped by for coffee and brought with her a determination to do something to help. Her contribution was to leave behind a hand-written Bible verse tacked above the sink. It promised, 'I can do all things through Christ who strengthens me' (Philippians 4:13).

Now, at one end of the phone was a poor woman who's world was caving in around her, not a piece of practical help around, nor a relative within thirty miles. And staring her in the face was a Bible verse telling her she ought to be able to cope. Christ's strength was all she needed. The friend's loving action, which was meant to open a window to heaven and to survival, had become a pit to disaster. Far from providing liberation and encouragement, that verse brought Rosemary condemnation and defeat.

So, doesn't scripture tell us that we can do all things through Christ's strength? If your answer is 'yes', let me ask you another question. Can you juggle? If not, please take four oranges. No, make that eggs. Begin to juggle, repeating that verse of scripture to yourself and trusting entirely in Christ to give you the strength to see you through.

Now take a few moments to clean up and read on.

Of course, that verse of scripture has nothing to do with juggling eggs — or eating fire, holding your breath for ten minutes, or memorising the works of Shakespeare backwards. Nor does it have anything to do with having the ability to cope with unreasonable demands or circumstances. Like every verse of scripture, it cannot be dragged out of its context, because that makes it say something different from what was intended.

When the apostle Paul wrote those words, it was in the context of saying, 'I have known what it is to have too much and I have known what it is not to have enough. I can accept having more than I need, and I can accept having less than I need.' Paul goes on to say, 'In every situation I have learned to be content. I can do all things through Christ, who strengthens me.'

That is the context. Paul is talking about coping with the need to have the right attitude — something very different from holding up the verse as a cure-all for every overwhelming situation. Sadly, we misuse this verse from the Bible constantly, allowing our wrong thinking to permeate our attitude toward people and circumstances. As a result, we feel condemned ourselves and we condemn others for not being spiritually together enough to cope with difficult times when they come.

If the strength of Christ was all we needed, then there would not be burdens for each other to carry. We would just be isolated, separate and self-contained believers with no need of each other. Come to think of it, isn't that just the way the church operates far too much of the time? Instead of being mutual supporters of each other, we abandon each other to a promise that is not a promise at all.

The central liberating truth of Paul's encouragement to us to carry each other's burdens (Galatians 6:2) is that this means it is OK to have burdens as Christians. These are not the burdens of those 'poor unfortunates outside the church who lack the resources of Jesus to see them through'. They are our burdens. It is an authentic experience for a Christian to have them and to do so is not a mark of being a substandard disciple. What is substandard and lacking in authenticity is to be part of a Christian community where you carry them alone.

In the same way we are called to 'weep with those who weep' (Romans 12:15, GNB). Again, this is the Christian community with tears in its eyes. One of the great promises of the Book of Revelation is that — at the end of all things — God will 'wipe away every tear from their eyes' (Revelation 7:17, GNB). And these eyes are the eyes of those who are his people, the church.

So allow me one simple question. Who should be doing the wiping of tears job until that moment? Right. Us. And that is the problem.

The greatest lie that the church tells is not with its voice but with its actions. We have not been called to follow Jesus as a collection of individuals who happen to meet together on a Sunday. We are not snooker balls, who click into each other just to head for our separate pockets for the rest of the week. Rather, we have been called together as a company of people to make a journey in dependence on one another.

But there is even more to it than that. Equally unfortunate is the fact that we in the family of faith so often also deny each other the right to have emotions — as I am about to explain.

Jesus allowed the whole of his person, including his emotions, to respond in the way it was designed. The emotions he expressed were not marks of sin and failure.

13

Can I have my emotions back, please?

We Brits have re-discovered our emotions. That is the way it looks from the surprisingly public expressions of grief that have been a feature of our national life in recent times.

Flowers in their tens of thousands. Weeping in the streets. A sense of reverence and sensitivity. All marked the aftermath of the tragic death of Diana, Princess of Wales. The British stiff upper lip has begun to tremble a little. To cry in public is no longer somewhat odd.

More recently, the epic film *Titanic* has also helped unblock our emotional drains. One major cinema complex actually obtained help from a tissue manufacturer who supplied free handy packs to distressed fans. Said the cinema, 'We just had to do something because so many people were bawling — even the men. Our staff have nicknamed it the "Crytanic".'

Historically, our society has not been good at grief. As the Very Reverend Dr Tom Wright said in a sermon preached in Lichfield Cathedral following Princess Diana's funeral, 'Mourners often suppress the natural, God-given emotion of grief. As a result, many carry around grief which they don't know what to do with. Diana gave us a chance to express it. Ironically, it was all right to grieve in public for Diana in a way that it wouldn't have been, in our heartless world, for a parent, spouse or child.'

A feature of this new trend in 'owning our emotions' was the gulf between those who did and those who didn't. Most notably senior members of the Royal Family themselves. Were they uncaring? Remote? In reality, they were simply part of a generation — don't forget how old they really are — which had been brought up to believe emotions are very private things. And certainly not to be worn on your sleeve.

Indeed, we British are very suspicious about emotions. We all know they are an integral part of the way we are made. Our problem is we all too easily lose sight of the fact — behaving as though it were not true. We would never feel guilty over catching measles, pulling a calf muscle, needing to wear glasses or having our appendix burst. But, quite irrationally, we do not always enjoy the same clear conscience when our equally God-given emotions malfunction.

OK to limp emotionally

Can it really be that depression is sinful but diabetes is morally neutral? Why is mental illness so often seen as a mark of sin and faithlessness when it occurs in Christians? As one who suffered commented, 'We know only too well the side-long glances, the patronising remarks, the spiritual exhortations, to which we are too often subjected; and they hurt.'

Why is it OK to take medication to control blood pressure, ulcers, backache and angina, but not to give relief to mental and emotional anguish? As Dr Marion Nelson declared in his classic but often unheeded book *Why Christians Crack Up*, published over thirty years ago, 'The idea that a Christian can know perfect mental peace at every moment is unrealistic and unscriptural. The fact is that Christians can suffer from any medical or psychological disorders that affect the rest of mankind.'[1]

We are led to believe that something not physical must be

spiritual. If it can be seen, it is physical. If it can't, it is spiritual. So if I break my leg, it is OK to limp. But if my heart is broken, and I 'limp' emotionally, it is essentially a spiritual problem.

Sadly, at the time of Rosemary's depression and stress, the answer in our church environment was that she needed to pray more, come to church more, read her Bible more. The symptoms were emotional. The solutions offered were all spiritual. Practical help was almost completely absent.

One of our friends made the cynical suggestion, 'Try breaking your leg. Then perhaps help will come.' Rosemary did — and help did come. To be factual, she chipped an ankle bone. But at least a broken ankle could be seen and understood. People rallied round. The cakes began to arrive and someone even did the ironing.

That incident left Rosemary observing it would be better to be on kidney dialysis than to suffer from depression. At least people would believe there was something medically wrong and not write it off as having its root in either the imagination or in spiritual inadequacy.

Being able to control our thoughts, we assume it ought to be possible to control our emotions. And we grow frustrated and disillusioned when we — and others — fail.

Unrealistic request

Worse still is when others expect us to respond to their encouragement, 'Pull yourself together.' That one phrase is the most thoughtless, cruel and unrealistic request anyone can make of someone operating under an emotional cloud. If someone could pull themselves together, then they most certainly would.

No one wants to wake up in the morning feeling as though some nocturnal cosmic vacuum cleaner had sucked every last ounce of joy from the universe. If there was a way in which someone could feel different, then they would grasp it with both hands.

There will be some who are alarmed because I view emotional distress as something to be accepted and responded to through a change in lifestyle and, when necessary, professional caring channels. To some, depression and other stress-related conditions should be the subject of spiritual warfare — to be rebuked and resisted.

There are times when this is true — but not often. Gifted and perceptive counsellors may very occasionally recognise symptoms as having their root in hostile spiritual forces or divine healing as being God's intention. But innumerable unfortunate people, believing they should have the same control over their feelings that they have over their limbs, have been offered instant miraculous release — only to be disappointed. They have incurred immense psychological damage as a result.

Even when we accept emotions as valid, there can be uncomfortable assumptions about their source. This could not be more strongly expressed than through an advertisement that caught my eye in an American Christian magazine. It asked ten questions which included: 'Are you too tired or unable to cope?'; 'Do you have problems with depression, anxiety or fear?'; 'Do you have trouble concentrating or remembering?' The answer to these predominantly emotional problems was summed up in the headline of the advertisement which asked, 'Could your problems be demonic in nature?' In other words, if there is something wrong with the way you feel, it could well be a spiritual issue.

Indeed, at a time when Rosemary was in the middle of some very dark days, a sincere Christian friend posed the question of whether the devil might be behind it all. Of course, Satan is at the root of the presence of sickness, death and disharmony in our world. But this is not the same as saying he or one of his crew are likely to be personally present when someone emotionally 'misfunctions'. To believe that is to misunderstand our own role in the cosmic battle.

Humankind are not a passive battlefield on which almost equal forces fight it out. The battle has already been won — with Christ as the victor. Satan only gains a foothold to affect our minds — or our bodies — if we open the door to him through some involvement in the occult. In which case, emotional malfunction is almost guaranteed to be accompanied by blasphemous thoughts without any remorse. A satanic dimension to emotional unrest will mix the classic symptoms of emotional illness with hatred and rebellion against all that is to do with God and the Christian faith. Without such clear signs we need to be looking for other natural explanations.

More than that, it is cruel and damaging to tell someone in the depths of emotional distress they are possessed by a spirit, without clear and overwhelming evidence this could be true. But the temptation to do so can be strong. This is because we may feel pressured to dismiss the psychological — which is not easily understood — as demonic. It may also be due to the need for simple and instant answers. And the longing to at least do something when faced with a seemingly impossible situation.

How God heals

My convictions fly in the face of those who seek dramatic and instant release from the symptoms of emotional illness. Of course, I do believe God heals people today. At times this is through him intervening in the natural laws he has created. But mostly, God heals through the natural processes that he has put within us. Cut your hand, break a leg, bruise a limb or catch a virus — and the body's natural healing processes automatically spring into action. Such events do not warrant calling for special prayer or reaching out to God for his miraculous intervention.

Most of us would be more likely to do handstands down the high street than to pray for instant deliverance from a broken leg. Faced with terminal illness or a condition that is beyond natural healing, that is the time when we will look to God to do what our body cannot. But our emotions equally are able to heal, as our bodies, given the right care and attention. So just as physical bruises and broken bones mend, so do bruised and broken emotions.

The Bible shows that God has emotions — including anger, compassion, regret and sorrow. As we are all made in God's image we share those emotions too. Far from being sub-human to have emotions, it is a mark of complete normality.

The Bible reveals some of the greatest expressions of human feeling through the psalmist David. We find him crying out in distress (Psalm 55:17), too troubled to speak (Psalm 77:4) and with a 'heart . . . wounded within me' (Psalm 109:22, NIV). He knew what it was to feel 'downcast', 'disturbed within', 'forgotten', in 'mourning', and 'oppressed' (Psalm 42).

The Lord Jesus proclaimed that those who experience the emotion of grief will be blessed. His promise was, 'Blessed are those who mourn, for they will be comforted' (Matthew 5:4, NIV).

William Barclay tells us:'The word translated mourn is one of the strongest words for mourning in the Greek language. It is used for mourning for the dead.' Barclay describes this grief as sorrow 'which pierces the heart . . . a sorrow which is poignant . . . and intense.'[2]

So Jesus is telling us we should not see an outward display of emotions as an indication of inner spiritual inadequacy. He not only approves of emotions, but says those who experience emotions of grief are blessed. We should not be surprised, because the Lord was no stranger to emotions himself.

At the tomb of Lazarus, Jesus was 'deeply moved in spirit and troubled' (John 11:33, NIV) and he wept. This was not for some super-spiritual reason or as part of a pulpit performance. It was an expression of his humanness over the consummate grief he felt for those who mourned the death of someone they loved. Nor was he play-acting when he was angry with the money changers in the Temple or when he wept over the city of Jerusalem.

If I am labouring the point, it is because it needs to be done. Too often I have seen the damage caused through denying Christians either the right to their emotions or permission for them to malfunction.

Understanding grief

This is seen most clearly in our own attitude to grief. Not everyone of us will experience emotional distress through stress and trauma. But we all eventually face the death of someone we love, if not the death of a relationship through divorce or the death of a meaningful existence through the loss of employment.

All too typical is the experience of a Christian couple who lost their fine teenage son in a car accident. When the news was shared with the church, it was also announced the couple 'had been wonderfully victorious. Not a tear. Just rejoicing that God's sovereign will has been done and Brian is now in heaven which is far better.' Nods of approval went round the church. Affirmation was given to the belief that 'victory' for the Christian means anaesthetising your emotions.

This 'don't grieve' idea may be due to a misunderstanding of Paul's words to the Christians in Thessalonica, where he told them, 'We do not want you to be ignorant about those who fall asleep, or to grieve like the rest of men, who have no hope' (1 Thessalonians 4:13, NIV). Paul is not giving instructions that the Thessalonians should not grieve. He is saying their grief should be of a different kind to that shown by those who do not have any hope. Far from condemning grief, he is actually approving it. But he is calling for a grief filled with hope rather than despair.

The older I get the more I find myself writing letters to those who have suffered bereavement. On those occasions I always encourage the recipient to try to see grief as a gift from God,

Understanding grief

Grief is the combination of sorrow, emotion and confusion that comes from losing someone or something important to you.

- It is common to feel numb, as though in shock.

- You mourn the loss and you mourn for yourself.

- You may experience tightness in the chest or throat, difficulty breathing, sensitivity to noise, the feeling that nothing is real, muscle weakness, lack of energy, dry mouth, or trouble with sleeping and eating.

- You may find yourself 'searching' for your loved one — through dreams which seem as real as life, and hallucinations caused by familiar sounds, smells and sights.

- Bereavement — the process of grieving — may last from six months to two years.

- You may find yourself angry at a person in particular or just angry in general, taking it out on those close to you. Try holding an imaginary conversation with the one you are angry with or write them a letter only you need see. Hit a pillow, kick a bed, or scream if it helps.

- Almost everyone experiences the guilt of 'I could have, I should have, I wish I would have'. If you feel your guilt is justified, write an apology — even if you are the only one to read it.

- Have at least one person you can talk through your feelings with. Or join a bereavement group.

- The time will come when you can think about your loved one with fond memories and without feelings of guilt, anger or sadness.

the outlet provided by the Creator for us to express our sense of loss. If the emotion of love is a reality, then grief is its expression at the time of passing and separation. It is to us what a valve is to a pressure cooker — the release is absolutely essential when our emotions are under pressure.

Several years ago I expressed this in a note to a young woman grieving the loss of her much-loved grandfather. In a brief but heartfelt note of reply, she said, 'Your letter arrived just when I needed it. I hadn't let myself cry. I guess I thought I needed to be strong, but I knew things were bottling up inside me. When I received your letter I felt such a release inside, and I was able to cry over the loss of someone I loved very much.'

Other emotions

Emotions of sadness and despair are not the only ones that cause problems to Christians. There is also the explosive experience of anger. Our difficulty may well spring from a confusion between 'losing our temper' and 'justifiable anger'.

We fail to note that there are more references in the Bible concerning God expressing anger, wrath and fury than there are of him expressing love. We wear blinkers to this truth, due to deep-seated belief that such an emotion must surely be sub-Christian.

God's anger is a reality — and we are made in his image. Anger is not part of our spoiled human nature — although when the two are put together it can be very bad news.

God, says the Bible, is 'slow to anger' (Numbers 14:18). And his anger 'lasts only a moment' (Psalm 30:5). This is demonstrated in the life of Jesus Christ. He wiped the floor with hypocrites and took a whip to those who used the worship of God to exploit others. He was angry at the lack of compassion of the Pharisees (Mark 3:5). But his anger was never out of his control.

For those of us who aspire to be like Jesus, there will be times when anger is justified. But this anger will be under control, mixed with compassion and brought to an end as swiftly as possible.

In reality, I know how hard this is. Which is why I tend to bottle up my angry feelings. Until recently, many counsellors would have encouraged the opposite. That we should let it all splatter forth. But new research shows this kind of behaviour can actually fuel the fires of anger rather than quench them.

Cool down

Professor Richard Winter quotes Murray Straus, a sociologist who has studied family violence. He observes that couples who yell at each other end up feeling more anger — because expressing anger can reinforce your attitude rather than expunge it. Instead, he advises, it is better to keep the lid on momentary irritations and to find distractions until you have cooled down. Then deal with the issue in a more calm and reasonable frame of mind.

There is every reason for us to be angry in the face of cruelty, greed, selfishness, injustice and the like. I particularly like Richard Winter's definition of three areas of life where the right kind of anger is justified. He sees these as being:

About injustice, cruelty, greed, arrogance and hypocrisy. Those issues which make God angry should make us angry too. If not, surely something is drastically wrong. Throughout the centuries such anger has been channelled by courageous men and women to fight for change rather than to brood over the way things are.

In relationships — marriage, friendship, children, colleagues. The husband who never listens; the child who constantly flouts parental authority; the in-law who is always mischievously interfering; the colleague whose ongoing laziness inflicts an unbearable burden — all deserve the response of appropriate anger.

Towards God. The Psalmist cried out, 'How long will you forget me and hide your face from me?' (Psalm 13:1). Just as he vented his anger heavenwards, so may we. God can cope with our anger and without it our relationship with him is less than honest.

Pressured prophets

It is essential to understand that it is truly valid for Christians to experience inner anguish, turmoil and pressure. This is not something reserved for the inadequate. A brief look at three major Old Testament prophets rams home something we tend to miss:they also had emotions and encountered pressure points of their own.

We stand in awe of Moses leading the people out of Israel, crossing the Red Sea and receiving the Law from God. Yet we are blind to his self-pitying protests that the people's constant rebellion and seething discontent had worn him out. We fail to note his pleas to God that he had reached the limit of his resources, requesting 'put me to death right now' (Numbers 11:15).

Hearts rise to Elijah on Mount Carmel, calling down the fire of heaven and destroying 450 false prophets. But the following day the same spiritual giant is fleeing from the threats of one woman. Exhausted from his spiritual conquest and a day's sun-beaten journey across the desert, he shelters under a broom tree and prays, 'I have had enough, Lord. Take my life' (1 Kings 19:4, NIV).

The prophet Jonah is not much different. Once we have the incident with the great fish behind us, we seem to progress no further than the triumph of his ensuing preaching crusade. But the sight of 120,000 people repenting in sackcloth and ashes led to an exhausted Jonah whose reputation and credibility was shot through. He had come to Nineveh warning that God would destroy the city. God had 'let him down' by sparing the people. Jonah's response was the anguished cry, 'It would be better for me to die than to live' (Jonah 4:8, NIV).

Emotions are part of our human make up. Everyone is subject to them, including God's greatest servants. It could even be argued that those most committed to God are most at risk.

Jesus — 'distressed'

If you still need convincing, look no further than the Garden of Gethsemane. There, facing the greatest ordeal that the universe has ever seen, the Lord Jesus tasted those emotions himself. As Mark records, 'He began to be deeply distressed and troubled. "My soul is overwhelmed with sorrow to the point of death," he said to them' (Mark 14:33–34, NIV). That is some expression of emotion:'deeply distressed' and 'overwhelmed with sorrow'. But if the Lord had responded in the way the British church can demand of its people, he would have put on the Galilean equivalent of the stiff upper lip and been sure to obey the instruction 'Don't let them see you cry'.

Instead, Jesus allowed the whole of his person, including his emotions, to respond in the way they were designed. The emotions he expressed were not marks of sin and failure. They were the normal outlet for someone overwhelmed by the situation he faced. Jesus had no need to reproach himself for the way he felt. Nor do we when distress, inner pain, sorrow and other similar responses arise as a result of the battles of life.

Finally, let's take one more look at Elijah, laying exhausted under a broom tree and despairing for his life (1 Kings 19:4). God's remedy is not a prayer meeting or some deep bone-shaking spiritual experience. Instead, God met his needs in four practical ways:

- first — sleep for refreshment (v 5);
- second — food and drink, for strength (vs 6,7);
- then — his own home — for familiarity and security (v 9);
- and finally 'a gentle whisper' (v 12) — the intimacy of his Creator's presence.

Note the order carefully. Our own solution would most likely have been to put the last first. But God knows that our ability to experience a sense of his presence can too easily be affected by our physical and emotional needs.

In the same way, the resurrected Jesus longed to say so much to his disciples on the shore of the Lake of Galilee. But the boys had been fishing all night (John 21:3). So first Jesus cooked them breakfast.

What all this means is, when our God-given emotions become subject to stress — and misbehave accordingly — we have no more reason to feel guilty and condemned than we do over a pulled muscle. And we have every right to expect the church to have the same attitude. Behaving as though we have no emotional dimension to our lives is to add a pressure point that should never have to be faced.

Having established the truth about our emotional make up, it is probably now about safe to look at that most painful of all results of stress, depression.

14

Don't mess with depression. It is a medical illness that must be diagnosed and treated by trained professionals.

Truly depressive

Depression — one of the extreme outcomes of stress overload — is a kind of emotional toothache. Rosemary saw it as an engulfing blackness in which life held all the joy of chewing sand — day after day.

Those who have not walked this painful path may imagine depression to be no more than simply feeling blue for a long time. Certainly, those who are depressed may have trouble sleeping, feel unusually sad or irritable, find it hard to concentrate and lose their appetite. They may also lack energy and have trouble feeling pleasure. But depression is far more than that — often leaving its victims simply no longer able to function in life.

Far from depression being 'all in the mind' it actually has physical causes. It is due to the brain chemicals serotonin and noradrenalin becoming depleted. This may be due to the impact of stress or changes in the body's hormones for other reasons. But it is why doctors prescribe anti-depressants.

Anti-depressants are not tranquillisers — aimed at subduing the patient — but a way of getting the brain working properly again so that stress management, relaxation and professional counselling can play their full part in recovery. Nor are they addictive.

Sadly, this does not stop people feeling ashamed at taking

them. Even though the same people would happily wear a support bandage while a weak ankle healed, or a cast so that a broken limb could mend.

According to official figures, one in seven adults suffer from anxiety and depression. Those most likely to fall victim are divorcees, women living alone, those who are unemployed and town dwellers in rented accommodation.

Women are particularly at risk, with one in four likely to experience severe depression at some time in their life.

The difference in how often depression affects women and men begins around adolescence — growing more pronounced with age, especially after 25. Between 44 and 65 years of age, the gender difference is less pronounced. But after the age of 65, women are again far more likely to be depressed.

Why the difference? One reason has to do with coping styles. Men are more likely to use action strategies whether they realise it or not. Work, sports, going out with friends — all distract them from their worries and gives them a sense of power and control.

In contrast, women tend to dwell on problems, often with

Symptoms of depression

- Exhaustion, fatigue and loss of energy
- Excessive pessimism, despondency, doubt and disenchantment
- Feelings of guilt, regret, hopelessness or worthlessness
- Eating disorder, changes in weight or appetite
- Sleep disturbance
- Suicidal tendencies, shame
- Irritability, indecision, inattention
- Negative thinking
- Obsessive behaviour
- Feelings of profound sadness or irritability
- Loss of interest or pleasure in activities once enjoyed
- Loss of libido and problems with sexual function
- Inability to concentrate, make decisions or remember simple things
- Aches and pains
- Restlessness or decreased activity noticed by others

other women. This is why exercise — especially aerobics — is a good partial antidote. It gives women an increased sense of self-discipline, control, and mastery.

Changes in levels of hormones such as oestrogen and progesterone also appear to have a strong effect on women's moods. This can explain why puberty, when many hormonal changes occur, marks the point from when women are more likely to experience depression.

Hormone levels also change during those events in a woman's life often associated with depression — including menstrual cycles, following giving birth, and the use of contraceptive pills which alter hormone levels. The 'baby blues' — the fluctuating emotions in the weeks following the birth of the baby — is also thought to be linked to plummeting levels of the hormones oestrogen and progesterone.

Panic attacks

Women not only suffer from depression more but it tends to be accompanied by other symptoms which occur more frequently in women, including anxiety, sleep and eating disorders and panic attacks.

Panic attacks — an overwhelming feeling of impending personal inability to cope, even that death was imminent — was Rosemary's worst experience. She fled from more shops, and left more supermarket trolleys abandoned than she could count. Yet, by taking her medication and getting good professional help it eventually became all in the past.

For some, the causes of depression is simply due to a lack of sun. Along with falling leaves and falling temperatures, go falling moods for up to one in five people, according to research from America. The condition has been labelled Seasonal Affective Disorder (SAD) — a lack of exposure to bright outdoor light.

As a result, multitudes each year face unexplained fatigue,

can't concentrate, withdraw from social contact, lose self-esteem, overeat, experience a drop in sex drive and, in some cases, face serious depression.

For those who can't head to the Bahamas, the answer is bright light treatment, called phototherapy. This involves about 20 minutes each day exposed to artificial bright light. This tricks the brain into thinking it is still summer, so reversing the hormonal responses that come to winter's dark days. For more information check out SAD on the Internet at www.geocities.com.

Early warning

It is unusual for depression to descend without some early warning signals. They are the kind of things covered earlier in this book relating to signs of stress-overload. If the response is a concerted programme of good stress management — lifestyle, relaxation, exercise, the right attitude and so on — it may well be possible to

Symptoms of panic attacks

You know when you have had a panic attack. But just in case you miss the symptoms, they are likely to include:

- shortness of breath or feelings of being smothered;

- dizziness, faintness or light-headedness;

- choking sensations, difficulty swallowing, or feeling something is caught in your throat;

- palpitations — feeling your heart is beating so hard it is will jump out of your chest;

- trembling or shaking;

- abdominal distress including cramp, nausea, vomiting or diarrhoea;

- numbness or tingling sensations of the hands and feet — and maybe the head or face;

- hot flushes or chills;

- sweating;

- crushing chest pains, feeling like a heart attack;

- fear that you are dying;

- fear that you are going crazy or going to lose control of yourself, or making a fool of yourself;

fend off the day of judgement. Although this may not always be the case where depression is the result of some overwhelming event or is hormonal rather than stress induced. In which case, good professional help is essential — through your doctor and the links this offers to psychologists and psychiatrists.

- blurred vision;
- headache;
- feelings of unreality, where things appear to be in slow motion, sounds louder or softer than you know they are, objects brighter or duller, or larger or smaller than you know to be true;
- depersonalisation — feeling that you are outside your body looking back at it.

You would expect that someone who had already experienced depression would more easily spot the signs the second time — and there will be one for over half of those who experience depression. But that is not always the case. Such people tend to attribute the new set of warning signs of fatigue and stress to the demands life is making on them.

Yet it is vital for likely victims and their families need to learn how to recognise the early warning signs. Because early action can prevent or reduce a further onset of darkness.

Research at the University of Michigan School of Nursing suggests that there will generally be at least one advance psychiatric symptom — anxiety, sadness, irritability, impaired work, decreased initiative, loss of interest, fatigue or insomnia.

The same research helpfully identifies four consistent warning themes which victims express in terms of:

1. *Something's not right*. The subjects of the research said they denied the symptoms, blaming their negative feelings on stress, the weather or other external difficulties, and used considerable energy putting up a front.

2. *Something's really wrong*. The participants' sleeping and eating patterns changed and their energy and the ability to

concentrate evaporated. They also withdrew from others, became anxious and even had thoughts of suicide.

3. *The crash*. Several pivotal symptoms develop, signalling the beginning of an acute episode of depression.

4. *Getting connected*. Getting connected meant seeking help from a family member, friend, or therapist.

An important sign of depression in older people is when they withdraw from regular social activities. Rather than explaining their symptoms as a medical illness, they tend to give excuses like: 'It's too much trouble', 'I don't feel well enough' or 'I don't have the energy'. For the same reasons, many neglect their personal appearance, or start to cook and eat less.

Christians too?

Above all, don't mess with depression. It is a medical illness that must be diagnosed and treated by trained professionals. Untreated, depression may last months or even years and can lead to disability, increase the symptoms of other illnesses, lead to premature death and even end in suicide.

Christians find it particularly hard to come to terms with the experience of depression. This relates strongly to how they view the world of their emotions, as we saw in the previous chapter. It is also because depression so clouds their spiritual experience.

Christians who are depressed find concentrating difficult. Reading the Bible and praying become tasks that are virtually impossible for more than a few minutes at a time. So unreasonable feelings of guilt become added to all their other emotional turmoil.

Dr John Lockley[1] observes, 'Depressed Christians are often a great deal nearer to God than they ever imagine. At the time when God appears to be far away, he is actually very close indeed; but because of the depression they don't perceive it.'

Jesus treated leaders as having physical and human needs. Too often we over-emphasise the supernatural dimension of the lives of our leaders. Each leader is expected to be an 'Indiana Jones' of the ministry.

15

What are we doing to our leaders?

The Bible had been read; a prolonged time of worship was over. Now it was time for some preaching. The circus-style big top was filled with some 4,000 people. The subject was 'The leadership of Christ', and I was the speaker.

The evening was part of a Spring Harvest week, an inter-church Bible-teaching event where pastors and lay people learn together.

Announcing my subject that night, I made a promise, 'This message is about leadership, but it is not for leaders. I am here to speak on behalf of leaders. It is time to understand how we are denying them the right to be the kind of leaders that God wants, producing more hurt, stress and pain for them than we can ever realise.'

Forty minutes later, towels, flannels and bowls of warm water were placed at points around the arena. 'The hands of many of our leaders are hard and calloused, symbolically speaking, from the work they have done. They are also tired and in need of refreshment,' I explained. 'For those of you for whom it is appropriate, please take this opportunity to wash the hands of your pastor — ministering refreshment, love and commitment.'

Within minutes, the vast crowd became a dynamic picture of the Christian life in action. Some formed natural small groups to pray for their leaders, repenting of the hurt and stress they had inflicted. Others washed hands, prayed, apologised, made fresh commitments. Many tears were shed; some whole churches experienced reconciliation, returning home with a new direction for the future.

I received a letter a few days later that was typical of the overwhelming response that came from the church leaders present: 'In my more than twenty years of pastoral ministry, I have never heard anyone address the needs of leaders as you did. It desperately needed saying. I only pray that my people who were there will understand and take action.'

It was no surprise that the message proved so relevant. A survey of British clergy revealed that one in three had seriously considered leaving the ministry. I also knew the number of Church of England clergy taking early retirement had doubled over the past four years. A US study of ex-pastors from the United Church of Christ showed that 68 per cent expressed that leaving the ministry left them feeling happy, more free, more rewarded, more human, more secure and more satisfied[1].

One United Kingdom denomination, the United Reformed Church, issued a report suggesting that two out of three illness among ministers may be stress-related[2]. That same report quoted a denominational training college principal as saying that at least one in ten of that denomination's ministers may show evidence of stress burn-out. Another study revealed that one in three pastors have taken time out due to emotional/stress illness over the previous three years[3].

Knowing all this, my task was to help the people I spoke to that evening see the kind of leadership that they desired and the kind that the Lord Jesus Christ modelled. My words had been based on the only miracle recorded by all four gospel writers — the feeding of the five thousand — and the emphasis each of them gives it.

Leadership is human

Mark's record of the feeding of the 5,000 shows Jesus taking his disciples away after an exhausting time of activity. The invitation was, 'Come with me by yourselves to a quiet place and get some rest' (Mark 6:31, NIV). The lesson is clear — Jesus treated leaders as having physical and human needs. Cut them and they bleed. Hurt them and they feel pain. Work them and they grow weary.

Yet, too often we over-emphasise the supernatural dimension of the lives of our leaders — their preaching, teaching, counselling and praying. Each leader is expected to be a 'Robo Cop' of the ministry. This is how we want them.

Our eyes are too often closed to the fact that Jesus took walks in a cornfield, enjoyed social meals, participated in a wedding, sailed a boat, rode a donkey, sang a hymn and cooked breakfast for his friends. Much of the pressure we inflict on our leaders stems from them being denied the same right of being human.

Leaders have emotions

Matthew's account of the bread and fishes miracle places it immediately after Jesus receiving the news of the death of John the Baptist, one of his cousins. To quote, 'When Jesus heard what had happened he withdrew by boat privately to a solitary place' (Matthew 14:13, NIV).

We see that the death of someone he loved brought Jesus emotional pain and loss. Jesus felt the death of John. Like our present-day leaders, he had emotions that could not be ignored.

I have already given examples of Jesus displaying his emotions. But note that we only know that Jesus expressed his emotions because his disciples were there to see it. He opened up his feelings to friends. Our leaders deserve that right as well. I am not recommending displays of emotional incontinence before whoever happens to be passing by, but our leaders need an inner group with whom they can be honest.

Leaders face pressure

Confronted with a huge and hungry crowd, Jesus turned to his disciples with the suggestion, 'You feed them!' Ultimately, they failed the test and put him under the kind of pressure we inflict on our leaders today.

'Send them away to solve their own problems' was the first proposal made by the disciples. There were no willing hands to ease the load. In our hurting world we all too often fail to be part of the solution — with the weight falling on the shoulders of the few who have the vision to make a difference. Leadership overload could be prevented if everyone played their part.

The disciples' second excuse was, 'That would take eight months of a man's wages' (Mark 6:37, NIV). The disciples didn't deny they had the money. Their argument was that it was an unreasonable request, simply too great a level of self-sacrifice to contemplate. Could it even be that for them to surrender eight months of wages to feed a crowd would have been more of a miracle than the one Jesus was eventually to perform? How painful for those with vision who are torn apart by the complacency and lack of commitment from the rest of us.

In the fourth gospel, John adds yet another dimension to the saga by recording the pressure Jesus faced when the miracle was over. Seeing the opportunity to enjoy free food for ever, the people 'intended to come and make him king by force' (John 6:15, NIV). They wanted Jesus for what was in it for them.

Our own leaders are confronted by this same attitude. Those they serve are more concerned with receiving than giving, with what they get than what they give. What matters is their taste and their best interest — all are of greatest importance than what they can contribute. Small wonder that our leaders are pressured.

Other sources of pressure

Yet all this is only a small part of the story. The stresses and pressures that bear down on the leaders of our churches come from a wide variety of sources. Many of the key factors have been well defined by John Adams and Roy Oswald of the Alban Institute[4]. They see them as:

Congregational expectations. The congregation — or sections within it — may have a different expectation of the role that their minister should fulfil when compared to his own game-plan. Or they may have unrealistic expectations of the range of gifts that any one person can have. Or they may simply be wanting someone 'just as wonderful' as the last incumbent.

Unclear job descriptions. Those in 'normal' employment benefit from clear Job descriptions and well-defined channels of authority. Too many local church leaders — particularly those still stuck in the one-man-ministry rut — are expected to do everything and to be answerable to everyone.

Such an inadequately defined role is likely to create a compulsive need to work even harder and harder in order to invoke the minimum amount of disappointment among those the leader is serving. That has to mean stress for anyone other than a sanctified Clark Kent.

Lack of pastoral care and loneliness. It is a vast understatement to say that the pastoral care of the pastors is woefully inadequate. Only fellow ministers really understand the pressures. Yet professional masks are kept securely in place and stiff upper lips are never allowed to tremble in the presence of others.

The few structures that do exist in order to make mutual pastoral care possible tend to do little to take relationships beyond the superficial, as a fly on the wall of almost any ministers' fraternal meeting will tell you. The overall result is isolation and loneliness.

Economic vulnerability. The generally low incomes of many pastors is a stress factor all on its own. The guilt that comes from inflicting his family with the pressure of 'the job' and from inadequate financial provision can be hard to carry. Added to that is the fact that the pastor's financial future and security is dependent on maintaining good relations within the church. They own your house, and this may be the only church you will ever get. Thus comes the stress of having to look over his shoulder constantly and listen for the distant hoofbeats of a vote of no confidence.

Time demands. The pastor is never allowed to be off duty. Even the most trivial of issues can occasion the words, 'I knew I would find you in, Pastor, seeing it's your day off.' There is also the interruption of emergencies. Some estimates indicate that 20 per cent of a pastor's time is devoted to emergencies or the unexpected. Just when he is more or less successfully managing to juggle an already unrealistic workload, someone will lob in a few surprises and bring the lot crashing down.

Adams and Oswald were also able to create a stress-relating scale of their own, based on the ministers' evaluations of how true for them a number of statements are, including: 'I must attend a meeting to get a job done'; 'I get feedback only when my performance is unsatisfactory'; 'I am fighting fires rather than working according to a plan'; 'I am stuck with the responsibility when a volunteer doesn't follow through on a task'; 'The congregation has role expectations for my spouse'; 'I arrive at work in the morning without a clear picture of where to begin'. These comments speak for themselves.

To the above we should add the observations of Enos D Martin, an American psychiatrist, who has made a study of depression in the clergy[5]. He cites several reasons for pastoral depression:

Complex role expectations. A pastor has more expected of him than someone in any other profession. As well as being under-paid and overworked, he must be a theologian, philosopher, businessman, politician, educator, preacher, public relations expert and counsellor. Yet his ministerial training is usually woefully inadequate in many of these areas. As a result, this complex set of expectations is matched by a sense of personal inadequacy.

Lack of firm roots. Moving from church to church is a standard procedure in ministry life — but it means losing the relationships which have become important to both the pastor and his family. It is a mark of the ministry that getting another pastorate just around the corner is simply 'not done'. The next job has to be a respectable distance away.

Unstructured counselling. Other professionals with counsel-ling responsibilities — psychiatrists for example — are able to work within a very structured setting. Their patients are seen for an agreed time and usually with a regular weekly time span between each contract. In contrast, the pastor can be called on at any hour of the day or night.

In addition, the minister is dealing with those about whom he cares deeply — and should he try to maintain a limit to this emotionally draining personal involvement, he can be accused of being uncaring.

In view of all this, it is hardly surprising that Ian Barclay, a former Churches Secretary at the Evangelical Alliance, describes the level of stress within clergy marriages as 'a big, big problem'. He estimates that in well over half of the parishes that he visits, those who are married and are in the ministry will look for opportunity to talk privately about the stress they are facing.

Nowhere to go. One of the major stress factors, he explains, is that for a minister to go to a superior with his problems could lead to a question mark over his future. So he may just bottle it all up and struggle on.

This fear of anyone knowing has been a motivating factor in the establishment by a Church Army Captain, Carl Lee, of a 'Samaritan-style' service for ministers and those in full-time Christian work. He has called it The Society of Mary and Martha[6] and has established a retreat centre to meet the growing needs of those hurt by the increasing pressures and faster pace of modern ministry. They offer a listening ear, practical help and wise advice, with skilled pastoral and professional help on hand.

It has been the escalating need among clergy marriages that had led to the 'Mary and Martha' project. The same conditions led to the United Reformed Church establishing a working party to produce their invaluable report 'Stress in the Ministry', which echoed the findings of its American counterparts that we have considered.

The report also observes that pastors can be held hostage by the standards they set for others. Having established a 'Christians don't have problems environment' — or inheriting one from the previous minister — they can face double trouble when problems become theirs. One pastor who had experienced depression is quoted as saying, 'There were even a few (in my congregation) who had the idea that as a minister I had no right to feel depressed or anxious about anything, and that all I had to do was pray and God would sort out the hitch and, really, where was my faith?'[7]

The leader's family

If things sound bad for men in the ministry, it can be even worse for their wives. The same report calls attention to the distinctive pressures that a minister's wife has to face. These include:

The expectation of others. Church members and the public

have their own 'image' of what life in the manse should be like
— and the wife has the pressure to fulfil those ideas.

Lack of privacy. The husband and family are always on call.
The needs of others must always be met even at the expense of
the needs of the minister's own spouse.

Finance. It is not merely the problem of finding ways to cope
on a low income that creates stress. It is also the issue of not
feeling valued, together with the conflict between needing to
be a home-maker and the pressure to take outside employment in order to make ends meet.

One minister's wife quoted in the report gives her own
summary of the stress that she and her compatriots have to
endure:

> The sense of isolation, lack of pastoral care either from the con-
> gregation or denomination, inadequate or badly maintained hous-
> ing, unrealistic expectations and demands placed upon the
> minister, his wife and the family, and the heavy burden placed
> on the wives of ministers to provide the major financial support
> of the family — all place immeasurable stress upon the marriage
> relationship itself.

Emotional needs. In addition to all this, Ian Barclay notes
that clergy wives face the stress of their husbands spending
extensive amounts of time in the company of other women
— while they are at home feeling neglected and having to
cope. He also cites the fact that many a pastor comes home
night after night too exhausted to meet the physical needs of
his partner.

On the same theme, Shirley Dobson, wife and co-worker of
Dr James Dobson, sees the sexual stress in ministry marriages
from another point of view. 'Women need the family specialist
to be emotionally satisfied before they can be sexually satisfied,' she explains. 'But men in the ministry tend to be so busy
and pre-occupied that their wives are emotionally neglected.

So when it comes to love-making, their wives have a tendency to feel used, cheap and unfulfilled.

All these problems are compounded by the fact that, often, the one person a minister cannot pastor is his own wife. When there is an organised pastoral care scheme within the church, it is unlikely that the minister's family will be on anyone's list. And the family are inhibited from asking for help — it doesn't go with the role.

Gender factor

I need to explain that my assumption that the minister is male and the spouse female is not the result of male chauvinism. Partly it is to avoid the complication of constantly using 'he or she'. My decision is helped by the fact that, still, by far the majority of those in the pastoral ministry are male. Had my subject been nurses, I would have felt equally comfortable writing about 'she', despite the presence of a considerable number of males in the nursing profession.

However, there is a far more important reason for the approach I have taken. The greatest levels of stress within clergy marriages occur when the minister is male. Reverse the roles and the male spouse is likely to be working and thus have a kinship group to shield him from loneliness. Meanwhile the congregation is unlikely to have preconceptions of how a ministerial husband should behave — so there is an absence of role-model pressures.

Nevertheless, evidence from the URC report suggests that single-women ministers face the stress of being expected to fulfil the role of both pastor and pastor's wife. Added to the responsibilities of preaching, visiting and the rest comes an expectation that they will also bake cakes for the church tea!

The stress that clergy wives face came to the surface when 400 wives of bishops attended the 1988 Lambeth Conference with their husbands. 60 per cent signed up for a workshop on the stress involved in living with a clergyman.

At the workshop was the wife of the then Bishop of Manchester, Mrs Anne Booth-Clibborn, a trained social worker. She says, 'If you are a doctor's wife, people do not come to you for a prescription. But if you are married to a minister, you are expected to be a perpetual source of sympathy and concern.'

We must not overlook the children of our ministers who also pay the price. I am told on good authority that a pastor received a phone call from an irate church steward asking, 'Why have all church meetings been cancelled?' Investigation revealed that a notice proclaiming that fact had been pinned to the church door. Further investigation disclosed that the culprit was the minister's son — who had not seen his father in weeks.

On reflection, I am surprised that this was an isolated incident. If someone were to manufacture 'all meetings cancelled until further notice' notices, they could find a booming market among ministerial families — and maybe start a welcome trend!

Leaders are vulnerable

My fourth point, drawn from the miracle of the loaves and fishes, centres on the reason that Jesus set the whole incident in motion in the first place. Matthew records, 'When Jesus landed and saw a large crowd, he had compassion on them and healed their sick' (Matthew 14:14, NIV). It was compassion that placed him centre stage in the drama of stress and pressure.

This reminds us that the qualities that make good pastors also put them at risk. A caring spirit, openness to others, sensitivity and empathy are actually the qualities that can make someone particularly vulnerable to the impact of stress. So pastors are not only subjected to excessive pressure points, but they are already particularly vulnerable to them as well.

Many of us never stop to consider that the way things are in our churches can create stress for those who have leadership responsibility within them. Tragically, our own lack of understanding then becomes yet another stress factor.

However bad all this sounds, please accept that it is actually worse than you might think. A poll of both pastors and lay people reveals that pastors are 50 per cent more stressed over finance and 100 per cent more stressed over their devotional life than their people imagine[8].

Worse than we think

Other areas where church members underestimate pastoral stress, according to this study, are time pressures, conflict issues, success pressures and housing. At the same time, the study shows that pastors are receiving only one-third of the level of support from their family that most members expect.

In her book *Coping With Stress at Work*[9], Dr Jacqueline Atkinson describes the symptoms of burn-out, the now well-accepted experience that hits mostly those in the caring professions. She lists the symptoms as including apathy, helplessness and hopelessness, overlaid with cynicism and possibly selfishness.

Dr Atkinson points out that: 'most people who suffer burn-out work within a bureaucratic organisation . . . probably underfunded and usually subject to cuts; they may have low pay and/or status, work in isolation with little social support, have reached career plateau with little chance of advancement and, most importantly, be faced with demanding clients and no clear criteria of success or even task completion.'

Does that sound like the ministry? Or does that sound like the ministry?

Dr Atkinson adds that the most common response to burn-out is to leave both the job and profession. This takes us back to almost the beginning of this chapter where we saw that eight out of ten who had left the ministry believe that they now have a better deal. Any of us with the power to affect the situation had better get to work — fast.

If we do not do something, we will be creating even more pressured pastors — like this one who wrote to me following my message on leadership. I'd like to conclude with his words:

> I am a minister and I came here on the edge of burn-out — physical, mental and spiritual. I was so badly off that I hadn't realised the problem. It was only on the second day, when attending your seminar on stress, that it dawned on me. Although the problem is still there, I have begun to get back in touch with God.
>
> The pressure had been so great. I had worked myself to a frazzle — teaching, leading, preaching, helping the Sunday School, playing the keyboards, leading the worship, running the house-groups etc, etc, etc. A lot of it is my own doing and I now have some idea of the area where I must say 'no'.
>
> What I am dreading is going home, to people who do not understand. I expect I am not the only leader here feeling guilty like this. I am just brave enough to admit it. So I pray that the members of my church who heard you speak on 'The leadership of Christ' last night will really take to heart that their leaders are human and do bleed — probably more easily than the rest of the members of the church. The problem is that we are so good at hiding it — often until it is too late.

16

*Our circumstances do not
tell us about God — it is
God who tells us about
our circumstances.*

Rejoice? Are you serious?

By reading this far, I hope you now understand where the pressure mortar bombs are likely to come from, why there are so many and why we are so often unable to cope. It is vital to accept that we are allowed to have problems and are not expected to cope with every dire circumstance. Yet, as Christians, we should also have clear understanding as to how God expects us to respond to the pressure points of life and where they fit into his plan for us.

As those born into God's family, we are not subject to chance, luck or accidents. The God who rules the universe equally rules our lives. He does not arbitrarily inflict adverse circumstances upon us, but neither do such circumstances catch him by surprise when they come. So how should we view them?

At the very moment I am writing these words, I should be at the silver wedding celebration of some great friends (who got married very young!). It would have been the first unhurried social night out for Rosemary and me in quite some time, and we had looked forward to it very much. Instead, I am in a hospital fifty miles from home and have just watched our fourth son, Zackary, return from theatre where they set his newly-broken arm. A mid-afternoon telephone call from the organiser of his Junior Church outing had prompted a swift drive and an equally speedy change of plans.

When the news gets out, we will face the usual sarcastic enquiries as to whether our family has shares in plaster of Paris — seeing that this is the third arm to be broken (all different children!) in less than nine months. The previous two came within three days of each other.

But what are we to make of the stress inflicted circumstances like these? How are we to respond when the world or the church lays yet another straw on our backs?

What God expects of us

It is in providing an answer to those questions that I find myself in danger of losing you as a reader — because God's instructions to those faced with the trials of life seem to be totally unrealistic. So unrealistic that, as I share them with you, you could find yourself saying, 'Who are you kidding?' and switch off completely to what follows.

What does God expect of us? Try this for size: joy. Or to express it more fully, 'Consider it pure joy, my brothers, whenever you face trials of many kinds' (James 1:2, NIV).

Can you cope with that? The dog has just chewed the new carpet; the twins have mumps; something sneaked into the washing and turned everything pink; and here comes a fanatic apostle called James, yelling through the letterbox 'Rejoice!' How unrealistic can you get?

Yet it is realistic — just like everything else in the Bible. God is telling us that wilfully to exercise joy in the face of adversity is the only adequate response we can make.

Yes, I know that sounds ridiculous. But before you throw it out, allow me to explain exactly why it is that James would have us respond to our trials with joy. Unreasonable as it seems if you can shelve your objections until you understand James's motivation, it can bring a completely new dimension to your life and help to deliver you from the resentment and confusion that too often accompanies such experiences.

What is meant by trials?

First we must put the command to 'rejoice when all kinds of trials come our way' into its context. A very bad accident, the death of someone close, redundancy, serious ill health — none of these are 'trials', unless you are incredibly thick-skinned and insensitive. These are all tragedies and it is not to events like these that James asks us to respond with outbursts of joy.

There are also events which most people may see as being merely a trial, but to us they are a disaster. It may be that these incidents either have some special significance or simply are the last straw. James does not call us to meet these events with joyfulness either. Such happenings bring forth the weeping that enables others to weep with us. So while we may, at first sight, view James's instruction as being unrealistic, at least we can see that he is not advocating masochism.

A 'trial' could be defined as a stone in the shoe of life — a circumstance that brings pressure and disorder without leaving us overwhelmed, or an event that tests our trust in God and causes us to question 'Why?' — that puts our faith on 'trial'.

Why should we respond to trials with joy?

There is a purpose

James says, 'Consider it pure joy . . . because . . . the testing of your faith develops perseverance. Perseverance must finish its work so that you may be mature and complete, not lacking anything' (James 1:2–4, NIV). The trials that come to us have a role to play, James is telling us. They have a reason and a purpose. They are to create the mature qualities of stickability and wholeness of character.

Not that each individual irritation is hand-picked by God in order to promote the fruit he desires. He does not plot

and plan to bring frustrations to us. It is just that pressures
and adverse circumstances — the stuff that real life is made
of — contribute to make us into more balanced and complete people.

The old Arab proverb puts it beautifully: 'All sunshine
makes a desert.' Certainly the most immature and barren
personalities are those who have sailed through life with the
sun always shining. In contrast, those for whom life has been a
struggle tend also to be the ones to whom others reach out to
when their own struggles come. They reach out with a confident expectation that they will be understood because someone has been there before and gained experience and maturity
in the process.

We should rejoice, James is telling us, because there will be a
glorious end result — the completeness of our character.

There is future reward

It is one thing to have a more complete character here and
now; it is quite another to receive a special reward when life is
over. That is what James is also promising. He explains,
'Blessed is the man who perseveres under trial, because
when he has stood the test, he will receive the crown of life
that God has promised to those who love him' (James 1:12,
NIV).

One of the marks of someone heading for a future life
with God is that they persevere under trial. When we see
ourselves bashing on in the face of adversity, it should cause
us to be joyful, because this is the evidence that we are on
the right road. At some later point, in a twinkling of an eye,
we will find ourselves on the winner's dais, the national
anthem of heaven playing, and the medals of victory will
be ours.

We rejoice because trials give us the opportunity to affirm
that our feet are on the road to heaven.

God does not change

When circumstances turn for the worse, our reflex action is often to feel that God has changed too. He is somehow less loving, less committed to us, less benevolent than he was when things were good. That is not how it is. James insists that God 'does not change like shifting shadows' (James 1:17, NIV). In effect, our circumstances do not tell us about God — it is God who tells us about our circumstances.

However bleak events may be, we cannot interpret them as telling us that God has ceased to be the loving, all-powerful, fair and extravagant heavenly Father that he is. Instead, because he is like that, it means our difficulties are in his control and his purposes for us are good.

God does not change. There is no danger that we may wake up one morning and find that he is no longer holy, just and good. Or that he feels vindictive and cruel. The Christian knows that God will never behave out of character. And we know what that character is like. James tells us, 'The Lord is full of compassion and mercy' (James 5:11, NIV). This is the stuff our heavenly Father is made of, even though the clouds of circumstances may hide that shining fact from us.

When fair winds are blowing in our direction, we have no problem in recognising what God is really like. I was present for the birth of each of our five children. Words can never express how good Rosemary and I felt God to be on every occasion. You can probably recall similar moments when God has seemed overwhelmingly good. He remains that good even when circumstances are not. He was still that good at the moment I hung up the telephone from speaking to the secretary of Rosemary's consultant, having been left with the belief that my life partner had only months to live.

No matter what befalls us or how high adversities pile up, the truth is that, in those moments, we are loved to the same extravagant extent as when the Lord Jesus gave his life for us on the cross. Our Lord is the same yesterday, today and forever. What he was yesterday, he is today and will be tomorrow — no matter what trials are ours.

Having a God like that is why rejoicing is in order.

Sitting here, in a strange hospital, with a child swathed in plaster, I must confess to finding myself somewhat less than joyful. Just contemplating sleeping on a put-u-up in the corner of a children's ward — compared with the comforts of home — is enough to stir up a tidal wave of self-pity. But I do know that the wilful expression of joy is what I should be aiming at — however short of that target I may fall.

James asks us to decide to rejoice. It is not something that is an automatic work of God's Spirit within us. If it were, James would not have needed to instruct his fellow Christians to respond to their trials with joy. And the fact that he had to give this instruction shows they were not making a decision to do so. So if you see yourself as being deficient in the 'rejoicing in trials' department, then you are in good company. The first Christians were not doing any better.

At those awful moments, when the mind is too numb to evaluate what is happening, I have discovered only one supreme source of comfort the knowledge that the Lord Jesus has experienced what I am experiencing.

17

When all else fails, hang on to Dad

Despite all the attempted wisdom and insight strewn across the preceding pages, I have to admit that there may be times when it is of no value at all. Such a time may not be the experience of everyone, but it may be for you or someone close to you.

Circumstances can become so engulfing that nothing makes sense any more and your brain is too battered to wrap itself around the theory of why you feel the way you do. It makes little difference whether you've reached this point because of one stark monumental hammer blow or a continued relentless barrage of adversity when the light at the end of the tunnel always turns out to be a train heading straight for you. The result can be the same — an inability to understand or respond with any sense of hope or purpose.

Rosemary and I have both faced situations like that at different times and in different ways. Many a tear has been shed as we met wave after wave of illness, misunderstanding, rejection and misadventure. Trouble in a dozen shapes and sizes has made its way to our door. At times we have been bruised, bewildered and battered to the point of almost despairing of life itself.

It is true what we have been through is nothing compared to the multitudes who have encountered crippling accidents, financial disasters, fatal diseases or loss of livelihood. Yet there is very little comfort, at a time of immense personal crisis, in having the head knowledge that there are thousands worse off than you. Perhaps it should help, but it turns out to be cold comfort when the heat is on. You may even find yourself feeling guilty for not being able to cope when there are others worse off than yourself.

At those awful moments, when the mind is too numb to evaluate what is happening, I have discovered only one supreme source of comfort — the knowledge that the Lord Jesus has experienced what I am experiencing. And the answer he found is enough for me too.

Jesus knows what it feels like

Come with me again to the Garden of Gethsemane. There we find the Lord 'deeply distressed and troubled . . . overwhelmed with sorrow to the point of death' (Mark 14:33–34, NIV). So great is his anguish that sweat like great drops of blood falls from his brow. However great my own inner turmoil and distress may be, I know that my Saviour can do more than sympathise from a distance. He can empathise because he has been through it all — and more.

The Lord Jesus has felt the pain of being abandoned, betrayed, exploited and pushed to the limits. He is not left trying to imagine what it must be like to be me when I am emotionally overrun. His own experience tells him exactly what it is like.

But even grasping the truth of that amazing statement may not be enough to see us through — and it doesn't have to be the limit of our resources. The response that Jesus made in his own hour of darkness is the ray of hope that can see us through as well.

There in the garden Jesus says, '*Abba*, Father' (Mark 14:36). That one word — Abba — sums up the key to our survival. That simple Aramaic word means 'Daddy'.

The Lord Jesus had already brought a new revelation about God to those who heard him. Until then they only understood God as the Father of their nation. Now Jesus spoke of God as a Father to individuals. But he reserves his own most intimate expression of his father-child relationship for his moment of greatest anguish.

We could be forgiven for imagining that the opposite would be the case. That it would have been moments of great spiritual ecstasy or triumph that ushered in such childlike abandon. On the Mount of Transfiguration, for example, or at the raising of Lazarus from the dead. But it is not so.

It is alone on a hillside, struggling with his whole destiny, that Jesus falls into the language of the nursery. Distressed, troubled, sorrowing to the point of death, Jesus responds with the word that he first spoke with dribble running down his chin: 'Daddy.'

That childlike expression, when spoken to God, expresses the simplest yet deepest truth that can be told. It was Father God who brought us to life by an act of his love. It is Father God who cherishes us with an overwhelming love. It is Father God whose plans for us are always in our best interest.

Circumstances may try to cloud the issue. But God is still 'Abba, Father' and worthy to be trusted with our bewilderment and doubt. In my own Gethsemane moments my response has been, 'Father, I know you are here somewhere. I cannot see you, feel you or sense your presence. But you are a loving heavenly father — and fathers do not abandon their children. So I am just going to keep on keeping on until the mists have cleared and I can see you again.' God expects no more of us than that.

Children can't always understand

It is the nature of a child not always to understand the reasons that fathers do things or allow them to happen. A recognition that God is 'Daddy' helps to bring that fact into focus. On one terrible African night, missionary Helen Roseveare was raped and almost killed. In the days that followed, with the question 'Why?' reverberating in her head, it seemed that the Lord came to her and said, 'Helen, can you still trust me even if I never explain why this happened to you?'

We tend to assume that everything can be explained, that we would be capable of understanding if only God would take the trouble to tell us. Yet, suppose some things are beyond our comprehension, that God is denied the opportunity to explain because it is not within our ability to grasp the meaning of what he would say . . .

Of all the traumas that have befallen our children, the one that haunts me the most concerns our third son, Aran, when he was about five years old. Running across our back garden at his frenetic speed, he tripped. Head and garden bench collided, badly tearing the corner of Aran's eyelid. One glance confirmed it was a stitches job and we made our familiar route to casualty.

The necessary stitches required a local anaesthetic, but the injection did not allow him to look the other way. The result was an agonising ten minutes while I physically held Aran down in order for the essential treatment to take place. There, wrapped in my arms and fighting tenaciously, his very best interests were being served. From his fearful and confused perspective, I was contributing to his pain. All he could say was 'Daddy' as we both cried together.

That is a picture of the way it has been, or will be, for many of us. If we could only see things from a different angle, we would find that God did know what he was doing, even though it made no sense to us. We would also see we were fully engulfed in his loving embrace. He was not sympathising from a distance, but personally and intimately involved in our experience.

For many of us, the heart of our failure to find peace under pressure is because we fail to grasp that we have a loving heavenly Father — who cares.

If we could see things from the perspective of heaven, perhaps we would even observe that we are not the only ones crying.

There are also tears in the eyes of the Father.

A discovery evening

Here are some creative ways to help others encounter the issues of stress. The suggestions provide an effective and imaginative evening to meet the needs of a home group as small as fifteen, or a church meeting of 200 or more.

Goals for the evening

- To help people understand the impact of stress and to take practical action.
- To affirm those who are struggling due to the impact of stress.
- To take people one step on in honest disclosure about themselves and their needs.

Ice breaker — 10 mins

Aim

To help people relax and be at home with each other while also introducing the overall subject of stress.

Method

This is an adaptation of a well-known party game, the details of which are hardly necessary. However, they are given just in case.

As people arrive give each person one half of a cloakroom ticket or ask them to write their name on a piece of paper which you collect and put in a small box.

On a table in the front of the room place a tray on which is a flour-cake topped with a £1 coin. (The cake is made by pressing flour hard into a mixing bowl and turning over with great care). Also on the tray is a knife.

Begin drawing people's names (or the other half of the cloakroom tickets) out of the box. That person must come forward to cut a piece off the cake without dislodging the coin. Proceed until finally the coin falls. The person responsible for this happening must now retrieve it with their teeth.

Immediately put people into groups of about eight. Ask them to talk about how they felt during the game. If their name was called, how did their body react? Compare feelings? Use this game to introduce the concept of stress.

Explaining stress — 10 mins

Have someone explain the basic principles of stress in terms of 'fight or flight' (see p. 14). Also to emphasise the current epidemic that has resulted from the levels of change, choice and chase (pace of life) in our society (see Chapters 3 and 4).

Group activity — 10 mins

Aim

To help people identify the balance that Jesus had in his life.

Method

Put people into groups of about five. Point out that during his three years of intense ministry, the Lord Jesus Christ managed to avoid burn-out. Ask them to list some of the reasons why this may have been. Give one or two examples of your own to get them going. Eg, he had a small group of close friends; he never drove on the M25 etc.

Feedback

Set about making a master list of answers on the OHP. Do this by having several groups read out up to five of their reasons — without repeating any that have gone before. Do not get caught up in arguing the merits of each answer. Just list the contributions without comment. Keep going until all the reasons are listed.

Teaching segment — 7 mins

Briefly explain the principle of the Life Change Units Scale and the particular impact that major change brings in terms of physical and emotional vulnerability (see p. 18).

Group activity — 10 mins

Aim

To help people to understand the implication of the Life-Change Units Scale.

Method

Put people into groups of about five. Explain their task as follows.

> On your answerphone you have found a message from your Christian friend Bill. Six months ago, he moved 200 miles away to work. Three months ago his father died. Two months ago he finally passed his professional examinations. A month ago his eldest daughter married. The message from Bill is, 'Everything is great. But . . . I can't sleep. I keep yelling at the kids. God feels miles away. I cry for no reason. I think I'm falling apart. Help!'
>
> What 45-second message would you leave on Bill's answerphone in reply?

You could copy out the question so that there was one for each group. Even better, put the facts about Bill on the OHP and play a tape recording of his frantic plea for help made by a suitable actor. Instruct each group to appoint a scribe who will write down the agreed message.

Feedback

Get the scribes from each group to stand up and then move on to another group with their message and read it to them.

Ask any group to indicate if they have heard a message which they consider is better than their own. Invite a selection of these high achievers to share the work with the whole crowd.

Group activity — 10 mins

Aim

To establish some practical things that people should do as a result of all they have heard.

Method

Keep people in their same groups of about five. Ideally, arrange for an extra chair to be added to each group. Alternatively ask people to imagine that there is such a chair. They are to picture Jesus sitting on this extra chair as part of their group.

The task is for each person to think what Jesus might want to say to them individually about the change, choice and chase of their lives. Tell them that they are to:

1. Use at least a minute of silence while people think.
2. Have each person in the group in turn say one brief phrase or sentence that reflects what Jesus might want to say to them.
3. Go round more than once if people have more to contribute.

4. Insist that people should not discuss what is said. They are only to say what they think Jesus might say — and listen.

Where you go from here will depend on how well those in the groups know one another and the measure of openness and trust between them. If they are acquaintances only it might be best to conclude with a time of silent reflection followed by a brief prayer. If there is trust and openness between them, a time of silence could be followed by people praying for one another in smaller groups of two or three.

Notes

Chapter 2

1. Based on TH Holmes and RH Rahe, 'The Social Readjustment Rating Scale', *Journal of Psychosomatic Research*, II, 1967 pp. 213–218.

Chapter 3

1. Quoted *Mail on Sunday* 16 November 1997.

Chapter 4

1. Statistics supplied by Credit Action.

Chapter 5

1. Richard Young, 'Stress Makes or Breaks the Man', *Sunday Times* (27 March 1988).
2. Dr Paul Bevington appearing in an interview on *Stress*, a six-part series by HTV, Wales (April/May 1988).
3. *Newsweek*, (25 April 1988), p. 32.
4. Quoted in 'Stress Makes or Breaks the Many', *Sunday Times* (27 March 1988).

Chapter 6

1. Dr Desmond Kelly, 'Fit to Cope with Stress?', *The Times*, 8 June 1989.
2. Quoted in 'Now say the TV isn't even relaxing', *Daily Telegraph*, 1 May 1990.
3. Gordon MacDonald, *Restoring Your Spiritual Passion*, Thomas Nelson: Nashville, 1986, p. 31.
4. Research by the Institute for the Advancement of Health in New York and by the American Association for Therapeutic Humor, quoted in 'Laughing Off Stress', *Daily Telegraph*, 29 October 1991.

Chapter 7

1. Richard Winter, *The Roots of Sorrow* (Crossway: Illinois, 1986).
2. Walter McQuade and Ann Aikman, *Stress: How to Stop Your Mind Killing Your Body* (Arrow/Hutchinson: London, 1974).
3. Ibid.

Chapter 8

1. Sullivan, Robert. 'Like you, I haven't been sleeping well', *Life*, (February 1998).

Chapter 9

1. *Aggressive Driving* by Louis Mizell, Bethesda, MD; *Road Rage* by Matthew Joint, MSc, BSc, MCIT UK. *Driver Aggression* by Dominic Connell, BSc and Matthew Joint, BSc, MSc, MCIT. Prepared for: AAA Foundation for Traffic Safety, Washington D.C. March 1997.
2. *Road Rage* by Matthew Joint, MSc, BSc, MCIT, the Automobile Association.
3. Research by RSGB published October 1997.
4. The Lex Report on Motoring by MORI conducted between 10 October and 18 November 1996.

Chapter 10

1. Quoted *Sunday Times*, 18 May 1997.
2. Commissioned by the *Sunday Times* and conducted by Professor Cary L Cooper of the University of Manchester Institute of Science and Technology. Quoted *Sunday Times* 18 May 1997.
3. Pritchett, Price, *New Work Habits for a Rapidly Changing World*, (Pritchet & Ass, Inc) 1994, p. 44.
4. Ibid.
5. Gallup/Institute for the Future/San Jose State University, USA. June 1997.
6. October 1966.

Chapter 11

1. Todd, Richard. 'Forever Young', *The Sunday Times*, 8 February 1998.

Chapter 13

1. Dr Marion Nelson, *Why Christians Crack Up*, Moody: Chicago, 1967 rev, p. 5.
2. William Barclay, *The Plain Man Looks at the Beatitudes*, Williams Collins and Sons: Glasgow, Fount, 1977, p. 25.

Chapter 14

1. 'When a Christian suffers depression' *Renewal* July 1997.

Chapter 15

1. G Jud, E Mills and G Burch, *Why Men Leave the Parish Ministry*, Pilgrim Press: Philadelphia, 1970.
2. 'Stress in the Ministry', London report by the United Reformed Church, 1987.
3. Keith Roberts, 'Pressure Points: Stress Survey', *Today* (March 1989).
4. John Adams and Roy Oswald, 'Ministry Related Stress', *Leadership* (Winter Quarter 1984), p. 95.

5. Enos D Martin, 'Depression and the Clergy', *Leadership* (Winter Quarter 1982), p. 80.
6. The Sheldon Centre, Dunsford, Exeter, EX6 7LE. Tel: (0647) 52752.
7. 'Stress in the Ministry', London report by the United Reformed Church, 1987, p. 6.
8. Keith Roberts, 'Pressure Points: Stress Survey', *Today* (April 1989), p. 40.
9. Dr Jacqueline Atkinson, *Coping With Stress at Work* (Thorsons: London 1988), p. 21.

Bibliography

Some useful Internet pages

www.cardinalpoints.com/stress
Includes a set of detailed self analysis questionnaires. An excellent resource and a lot of fun.

www.teachhealth.com/
A useful overview of stress and how to respond

www.extension.umn.edu/Documents/H/E/HE1005.html
A mass of stress related material — covering: 'Helping Children Cope With Stress', 'Coping With Job Loss', 'Helping Others In Distress', 'Coping With Loss And Grief', and even 'Stress On The Farm'.

www.algy.com/anxiety/about.html
A grass roots project involving thousands of people interested in anxiety disorders such as panic attacks, phobias, shyness, generalised anxiety, obsessive-compulsive behaviour and post traumatic stress.

Books/publications

Adair, John, *How to Manage Your Time*, Talbut Adair, 1988.
Atkinson, Jacqueline M, *Coping With Stress at Work*, Thorsons Publishing Group, 1988.

Back, Ken and Kate, *Assertiveness at Work*, McGraw-Hill, 1982.

Bull, Stephen, *Sports Psychology: A Self-Help Guide*, Crowood Press.

Butt, Dorcas, *Psychology of Sport: Behaviour, Motivation, Personality and Performance of Athletes*, Van Nost Reinhold.

Cartwright, Susan and Cooper, Gary L, *Managing Workplace Stress*, Sage.

Coleman, Dr Vernon, *Overcoming Stress*, Sheldon Press, 1988.

Davies, Gaius, *Stress: the Challenge to Christian Caring*, Kingsway, 1988.

Davidson, Geoff, *The Complete Idiot's Guide to Managing Stress*, Alpha Books, 1997.

Dickson, Anne, *A Woman in Your Own Right — Assertiveness and You*, Quartet, 1987.

Fletcher, Dr Ben C and MacPherson, Rev. David, *Stress Among Parochial Clergy in the Church of England*, Hatfield Polytechnic, 1989.

Ghazi, Polly and Jones, Judy, *Downshifting — The Guide to Happier, Simpler Living*, Coronet, 1997.

Galer, Anne and Pratt, D Alasdair, *Stress in the Ministry*, United Reformed Church, 1987.

Hannaway, Conor and Hunt, Gabriel, *The Management Skills Book*, Gower, UK, ISBN 0–556–07283–1.

Horsman, Sarah, *Living With Stress — A Guide for Christian Ministers*, Society of Mary and Martha, 1987.

Jones, Dr Alfred, *Stress Management*, Stress Control Products Ltd, 1988.

Kirsta, Alix, *The Book of Stress Survival*, Thorsons/Harper Collins, UK, ISBN 0–7225–2592–3.

Lewis, Dr David, *10 Minute Time and Stress Management*, Piatkus, UK, ISBN 0–7499–1428–6.

Madders, Jane, *Relax — The Relief of Tension Through Muscle Control*, London BBC, 1973.

McKenna, Regis, *Real Time*, Harvard Business School Press, 1997.

Nelson, Marion H, *Why Christians Crack Up*, Moody, 1967.

Orlick, Terry, *In Pursuit of Excellence*, Human Kinetics, US, 0–88011–380–4/.

Price, Pritchett, *New Work Habits for a Radically Changing World*, 1994.

Rowland, Val and Birkett, Ken, *Personal Effectiveness for Teachers*, Simon & Schuster Education, UK, ISBNO 7501 01857.

Rush, Myron, *Burn-out*, Scripture Press, 1989.

Sharpe, Robert, *Assert Yourself*, Kogan Page, 1989.

Selye, Hans, *The Stress of Life*, McGraw-Hill, 1956, revised ed, 1976.

Thompson, Dr Dick, *Pocket Guide to Stress and How to Live With It*, Arlington Books, 1982.

Toffler, Alvin, *Future Shock*, Random House Inc, 1970.

Wilkinson, Dr G Coping With Stress, London Family Doctor Publications, 1987.

Articles/Features

Adams, John and Oswald, Ron, 'Ministry-related Stress', *Leadership*, Winter quarter, 1980.

Ahlbom, A, Baker, D, Karasek, RA, Marxer, F and Theorell, T, 'Job Decision attitude, Job Demands and Cardiovascular Disease: A prospected study of Swedish men', *American Journal of Public Health 71: 694—705, 1981*.

Allen-Mills, Tony, 'Don't sleep on it', *The Sunday Times*, March 1998.

Breecher, Mawry M, 'Six Ways to Get Un-depressed', *Complete Woman*, 1988.

Cirsta, Alix, 'Relax! A Positive Approach to Stress', *Woman's Journal*, August 1988.

Clements, Anna, 'Why is everyone always so tired?', *Woman's Own*, 2 February 1998.

Cohen, Nick, 'Let's all weep together', *The Observer*, 9 November 1997.

Daniels, Alison, 'Stress takes toll on office staff', *The Guardian*, 21 October 1997.

Denison, Simon, 'Laughing Off Stress', *Daily Telegraph*, 29 October 1991.

Grice, Elizabeth, 'Stress Makes or Breaks the Man', *Sunday Times*, 27 March 1988.

Jones, Michael, 'The Stressed Doctor in a Stressful Society', *Journal of the Christian Medical Fellowship*, April 1988.

Lane, Barbara, 'Fit to Cope with Stress?' *The Times*, 8 June 1989.

Levoy, Gregg, 'Tears that Speak', *Psychology Today*, July 1988.

Littleton, Mark R, 'Depression in the Clergy', *Leadership*, Winter quarter, 1984.

Lockley, Dr John, 'When a Christian suffers depression', *Renewal*, July 1997.

McBride, Michael G, 'The Vocational Stress of Ministry', *Ministry*, January 1989.

McBride, Michael G, 'Managing Ministerial Stress', *Ministry*, March 1989.

Moss, Professor Rowland, 'Stress and Depression — A Personal Experience', *Christian Arena*, June 1984.

Overstress, R Larry, 'After the Funeral', *Moody Monthly*, May 1981.

Roberts, Keith, 'Pressure Points/ Stress Survey', *Today*, March 1989.

Robert, Keith, 'A View from the Pews/Stress Survey', *Today*, April 1989.

Rosner, Bob, 'How do you deal with information overload?', *The Costco Connection*, Winter 1997.

Stanway, Roger, 'Stress — The Missing Dimension', *The Network Papers Vol I, No 8*, 1990.

Sullivan, Robert, 'Like you, I haven't been sleeping well', *Life*, February 1998.

Todd, Richard, 'Forever Young', *The Sunday Times*, 8 February 1998.

Tucker, Ruth A, 'Working Mothers', *Christianity Today*, 15 July 1988. 'Stress on the Job', *Newsweek*, 25 April, 1988.

Uhllig, Robert, 'Office workers sinking under tide of technology', *Daily Telegraph*, 24 June 1997.

Worth, Jill, 'The Particular Hell', *Today*, May 1990.